The Observer's Pocket Series

OPERA

About the book

Opera is a form of theatre, and the aim of this book is to increase the enjoyment of opera by adding to the opera-goer's understanding of the history behind the work performed as well as the story being dramatized. Opera composers are listed alphabetically, with notes on their lives and works. The stories of their major operas—and many of those less frequently performed—are recounted in each entry. There is a comprehensive index to all the operas mentioned in the book.

About the author

Elizabeth Forbes, a freelance writer on music, has been passionately addicted to opera for many years and considers herself extraordinarily lucky in that much of her job consists of doing just what she most enjoys—that is, going to the opera. She finds that opera, with its combination of singing, orchestral music, drama and spectacle (often including ballet), is the most satisfying form of theatre. Thirty years of assiduous opera-going in Britain, Europe and the United States have in no way blunted her appetite, either for the fiftieth performance of *Madam Butterfly* or *La traviata* or for the first production of a brand-new opera. Her work as translator of several opera texts has reinforced her belief that opera is not just a collection of gorgeous voices making a series of more or less lovely sounds, but a vital and enjoyable theatrical experience.

The Observer's Book of
OPERA

ELIZABETH FORBES

WITH 27 BLACK AND WHITE PHOTOGRAPHS

FREDERICK WARNE
LONDON

Published by
Frederick Warne (Publishers) Ltd, London 1982
© Elizabeth Forbes 1982

ISBN 0 7232 1638 X

Typeset by CCC, printed and bound by
William Clowes (Beccles) Limited,
Beccles and London

CONTENTS

Foreword	6
A Brief History of Opera	7
Composers and Their Works	13
Bibliography	182
Index to Operas	184

FOREWORD

The sole object of this book is to try to help the potential opera-lover derive as much enjoyment as possible from a form of theatre that can offer more pleasure than any other. I stress the words 'form of theatre' because opera, being a mixture of song, orchestral music, drama, scenic design and, frequently, dance, is the most theatrical of the performing arts.

Because it combines so many different ingredients, an operatic production can very easily go wrong or fail in one of its elements. But on those rare occasions when everything goes magnificently right, the experience generates a satisfaction of correspondingly great intensity. A little extra knowledge of the subject increases that satisfaction even more.

A BRIEF HISTORY OF OPERA

Opera can claim to have been born in 1597, the date when Jacopo Peri's *Dafne* was performed in Florence by the *Camerata*. The *Camerata* was a society of musicians and poets whose attempts to re-create the fusion of words and music in ancient Greek drama, as they imagined it, led to the creation of a new art form. The real roots of opera lie not in Greek drama, but in the sacred mystery or miracle plays and the secular pastorals and masques, which contained singing, dancing and spectacle, performed in the princely courts of Europe.

The subjects of the earliest operas were taken from Greek mythology, like *Dafne* or Peri's *Euridice* (1600), the first opera to survive, while words were given prominence over music. The new entertainment spread rapidly, to the Italian courts, such as Mantua, where Monteverdi was Master of Music to the Duke, and to the cities, such as Venice, where the first public opera house opened in 1637. Opera became a craze in Venice; several more theatres opened and works by Monteverdi, Cavalli and other composers achieved great popularity.

A third ingredient, spectacle—which included dance—joined the original dramatic mixture of words and music, and the history of opera ever since can be charted by the relative importance allotted to each element at different periods. The fluidity of form characteristic of the earliest operas gradually congealed into the rigid conventions of *opera seria*, whose serious libretto, or text, was required to have a happy ending, while its music was sharply divided into aria, or song, and recitative, or declamation. Although the first half of the eighteenth century was an epoch when the musical, or more exactly the vocal, aspect of opera was in the ascendancy, one of the key figures of the period was paradoxically the poet Pietro Metastasio, whose numerous texts were each set by many composers.

By then Naples had replaced Venice as the Italian operatic centre, and it was in Naples that the next significant development took place. Comic *intermezzi* or interludes were often inserted into serious operas as a contrast to their high-minded sentiments and exclusive concentration on persons of royal or divine blood. These interludes became so popular that they were performed on their own. *Opera buffa*, or comic opera, dealt with the dilemmas of ordinary people, not of kings and gods, and the most famous of the interludes, Pergolesi's *La serva padrona* (The Maid Mistress), even sparked off the so-called *Guerre des Bouffons* (War of the Comedians) in Paris.

French taste, influenced by the gorgeous court entertainments of Louis XIV and XV, inclined towards the spectacular. The operas of Lully and, later, Rameau, with their emphasis on this aspect of the drama, were especially popular. But some performances of *La serva padrona* by a troupe of comedians proved so successful that society and public opinion were split into two opposing camps.

In northern Europe, Italian opera reigned in the court theatres, but an indigenous product also began to appear. The German *Singspiel*, in which spoken dialogue replaced the recitative of Italian opera, had gained a firm footing by the beginning of the eighteenth century. In England the masque, as exemplified by Arne and Purcell, and the ballad-opera provided popular alternatives to Italian serious opera, which attained its greatest success during the earlier part of Handel's long domicile in London. In *The Beggar's Opera*, which symbolized the reaction against the dramatic absurdities of Metastasian opera, Pepusch borrowed music from

Handel for his arrangements of popular tunes of the day.

In Vienna, the revolt against the long tyranny of operatic singers, in particular the *castrati*, or male sopranos and altos, who dominated the stage, was led by Gluck, who had himself set several of Metastasio's texts. Gluck tried to integrate the various elements of opera more closely and to abolish vocal display for its own sake, advocating, in fact, a return to the ideals of the *Camerata*. Mozart also breathed new life into *opera seria* and, though no innovator, re-animated both Italian comic opera and German *Singspiel* with his genius. In *Fidelio*, technically a *Singspiel*, Beethoven too transcended the limits of the genre.

But the pendulum was due to swing again. The Romantic movement in literature, originating in Germany, rapidly spread to other arts and other countries, in particular to Italy. While the operas of Rossini, both serious and comic, have a classical elegance and style, those of Bellini and of Donizetti, when in tragic mood, show a Romantic tendency to exceed the bounds of reason and moderation. The novels of Sir Walter Scott, which appeared in translation throughout Europe, were used as the basis for many an opera plot, and the colourful figures of British history also provided excellent operatic material. Shakespeare, hitherto frowned upon in Latin countries, became immensely popular, though only Verdi among Italian opera composers could match his genius.

In France, surrender to the Romantic movement was delayed by the French admiration for classical drama as written by Corneille and Racine, and for the operas of Gluck and Spontini composed for the Paris Opéra. But the notorious first performance of Victor Hugo's play *Hernani* in 1830 opened the door wide to Romanticism and also to grand opera, a specifically French form of musical drama in which spectacle and ballet were of particular importance. These were typified by the French operas of Meyerbeer, with their historical backgrounds, enormous casts and grandiose tableaux. As a popular alternative to the Meyerbeerian juggernauts, *opéra-comique*—not necessarily comic, but with spoken dialogue—was provided by Auber, Hérold and many others.

German Romanticism is to be found in its purest form in the operas of Weber who, together with Marschner, exerted a great influence on the earlier works of Wagner. Wagner dominated German opera throughout the second half of the nineteenth century. His conception of the *Gesamtkunstwerk*, or unified work of art, as well as the enormous scale of his compositions, forced him to build his own theatre at Bayreuth, where his music dramas could be performed under ideal conditions.

Wagner's influence, felt throughout Europe, was particularly strong in France. Some French composers, such as Saint-Saëns and Fauré, adapted his musical language to their own styles. Others, such as Debussy, reacted violently against his precepts. A few, including Massenet, were sufficiently detached to take what they needed from Wagner's theories and reject the rest. Many twentieth-century French opera composers, including Ravel and Poulenc, have tended to follow Debussy in reacting against the German influence.

The latter part of the nineteenth century witnessed the rise of nationalist opera in several countries without an operatic heritage of their own. In Russia the pioneering works of Glinka, in which the Italian influence was still perceptible, were followed by the wholly Russian operas of Mussorgsky, Borodin and Rimsky-Korsakov. Tchaikovsky, more cosmopolitan in outlook, showed the impact of French and German styles on his operas. Czechoslovakia, though still at that time part of the Austro-Hungarian Empire, was rich in nationalist composers. Both Smetana and, to a lesser degree, Dvořák were accused of succumbing to Wagnerism but their successor, Janáček, evolved a style wholly his own that flowered with amazing vitality in the last decade of his life.

Meanwhile in Italy, dominated for half a century by Verdi, a new operatic style was emerging, that of *verismo* or realism, in which the violent emotions of ordinary people were put, as it were, under the microscope. Mascagni, Leoncavallo and Giordano wrote popular veristic works. A second, even more emotional wave of post-veristic composers included Montemezzi, Zandonai and Wolf-Ferrari. Puccini, frequently labelled with the tag of *verismo*, had in fact a much wider range. Since his death in 1924 no new, really popular operatic composer has emerged in Italy. Menotti, though Italian by birth, has pursued his career mainly in the USA and must be counted as an American composer.

German opera in the first half of the twentieth century was overshadowed by Richard Strauss, in retrospect the last of the Romantics rather than the first of a new generation. Strauss extended tonality, or musical composition based on the key system, to its limits in *Elektra*. He then retreated, leaving Schoenberg and Berg to adapt the former's dodecaphonic or 12-tone system to opera. This dispenses with keys altogether, using instead all the 12 notes in the scale. In the 1950s Henze emerged as a major operatic talent, with an instinct for the theatre unique among his contemporaries.

The English musical renaissance at the turn of the century was mainly symphonic, but Delius and, later, Vaughan Williams stand out as interesting, if not wholly successful, opera composers. It was left to Britten in the period immediately following World War II to found a school of British opera almost single-handed. Tippett has also added significantly to the repertory of British opera, though the obscurity of his texts, which he writes himself, precludes the kind of popular success that Britten has won.

Meanwhile the pendulum continues to swing. Romantic opera opened the way to another epoch dominated by the singer. Growing complexity in the orchestral part, culminating in the colossal scores of Wagner and Strauss, led to the rise of the star conductor. Today, with emphasis on the dramatic aspect, the producer rules supreme. Opera, whose death has so frequently been forecast, approaches its 400th birthday with lively confidence.

Note
Characters are assigned their voice categories as follows:
Soprano: highest pitched female voice
Mezzo-soprano: middle pitched female voice
Contralto: lowest pitched female voice
Tenor: highest pitched male voice
Baritone: middle pitched male voice
Bass: lowest pitched male voice
Treble: boy's voice corresponding to soprano
Counter-tenor: male voice corresponding to mezzo-soprano

COMPOSERS AND THEIR WORKS

Adam, Adolphe (1803–56), French composer. His serious career began in 1829 with the production of *Pierre et Catherine* at the Opéra-Comique, Paris. Though best remembered now for his ballet *Giselle*, Adam wrote several operas that were enormously successful at the time, in particular *Le Chalet* (1830), a one-acter that reached its 1,500th performance at the Opéra-Comique in 1922, and *Le Postillon de Longjumeau*, with text by A. de Leuven and L. L. Brunswick, first performed on 13 October 1836 at the same theatre.

Alfano, Franco (1876–1954), Italian composer. Although best remembered for his completion of the third act of Puccini's *Turandot*, Alfano wrote a number of operas himself. The most successful are *Risurrezione*, an adaptation of Tolstoy's novel *Resurrection*, first performed at Turin in 1904, and *Cyrano de Bergerac*, after the play by Rostand, produced at Rome in 1936.

Arne, Thomas (1710–78), English composer. A prolific writer of masques, such as the adaptation of Milton's *Comus* (1738) and *Alfred* (1740) (which contains 'Rule Britannia'), as well as many popular operas, including *Thomas and Sally* (1760) and *Love in a Village* (1762). He also composed *Artaxerxes*, an opera in the Italian style, with text translated from Metastasio, and sung recitative replacing dialogue, first produced in 1762 at Covent Garden.

Auber, Daniel (1782–1871), French composer. He scored his first public success in Paris with *La Bergère châtelaine* (1820) at the Opéra-Comique. His next opera,

Leicester, ou le Château de Kenilworth, an adaptation of Walter Scott's novel, inaugurated a 40-year collaboration with the librettist Eugène Scribe, who, alone or in collaboration, provided the composer with 37 texts. These include *La Muette de Portici* (1828) and *Fra Diavolo* (1830), Auber's two best-known operas, as well as *Gustave III ou le Bal masqué* (1833), *Le Cheval de bronze* (1835), *Le Domino noir* (1837), *Les Diamants de la couronne* (1841) and *Manon Lescaut* (1856), all of them highly popular at the time.

Balfe, Michael (1808–70), Irish composer. After a successful career as a singer (baritone) in Paris and Italy, Balfe returned to London in 1835, when his opera *The Siege of Rochelle* was given at Drury Lane, followed by *The Maid of Artois* (1836). *Falstaff* (1838) was given in Italian at Her Majesty's Theatre. Balfe's best-known opera, *The Bohemian Girl* (1843), retained its popularity for three-quarters of a century. His last opera, *The Knight of the Leopard*, an adaptation of Scott's novel *The Talisman*, was produced posthumously at Drury Lane in 1874, sung in Italian as *Il talismano*.

Barber, Samuel (1910–81), American composer. His first full-length opera, *Vanessa*, with text by Gian-Carlo Menotti, was first produced in 1958 at the old Metropolitan, New York. His second, *Antony and Cleopatra*, from Shakespeare's play, opened the new Metropolitan Opera House in Lincoln Center, in 1966.

Bartók, Béla (1881–1945), Hungarian composer. His only opera, *Duke Bluebeard's Castle*, though composed in 1911, was not performed until seven years later.
Duke Bluebeard's Castle, opera in one act, with text by Béla Balácz, first performed on 24 May 1918 at Budapest.

A room in Bluebeard's castle, with a staircase

descending from a small iron door. There are no windows but seven larger doors, all locked. Bluebeard (bass) leads his bride Judith (mezzo-soprano) down the staircase. Finding the castle gloomy, she wishes to open the seven doors. After some argument, Bluebeard gives her the keys for the first five doors. The first reveals the torture chamber, red with blood; the second, an armoury; the third, the treasury filled with jewels, from which she takes a cloak and a crown; the fourth, a garden, with flowers also stained in blood; the fifth, a vast panorama over Bluebeard's kingdom. At first Bluebeard will not give her the last two keys, but Judith is adamant, and finally he yields. The sixth door opens on a lake of tears. When the last door is opened, three beautiful women appear through it. They are Bluebeard's previous wives, the first embodying the morning of his life, the second the noonday, the third the afternoon, while Judith herself embodies the night. The three wives return through the seventh door, followed by Judith wearing the crown and cloak from the treasury. The door closes after her, and Bluebeard is alone.

Beethoven, Ludwig van (1770–1827), German composer. Beethoven completed only one opera, *Fidelio*, which caused him an enormous amount of trouble, being revised twice over a period of ten years. Despite this, he continued to search for another suitable operatic subject for the rest of his life, unfortunately without success.

Fidelio, opera originally in three acts, with text by Josef Sonnleithner, based on Bouilly's libretto *Léonore, ou l'amour conjugal*, first produced on 20 November 1805, at the Theater an der Wien, Vienna. Revised version in two acts produced on 29 March 1806 at the same theatre. Final version, text revised by G. F. Treitschke, first produced on 23 May 1814 at the Kärntnertortheater, Vienna. Based on an incident that supposedly took place in France during the Revolution, the action of *Fidelio* has been transferred to eighteenth-century Spain.

ACT 1. After the overture (Beethoven composed four altogether: *Leonore* 1, 2, and 3, and the *Fidelio* overture usually played today) the curtain rises on the courtyard of a prison-fortress near Seville. Marzelline (soprano), daughter to the chief jailer Rocco (bass), and Jacquino (tenor), his assistant, are quarrelling; Jacquino wants to marry Marzelline, but she has fallen in love with Fidelio, who also helps her father with the prisoners. Fidelio is in fact Leonore (soprano), who is searching for her husband Don Florestan, whom she believes to be imprisoned in the fortress. In a quartet she, Marzelline, Jacquino and Rocco express their secret thoughts. Rocco favours a marriage between his daughter and Fidelio, though he warns them that money is needed as well as love. He agrees to ask the governor, Don Pizarro, for consent to the marriage, and for Fidelio to be allowed to help him more with the prisoners.

Don Pizarro (bass) reads his despatches, which include an anonymous warning that a minister of state is coming from Seville to verify a rumour that his friend Florestan, long thought dead, is secretly incarcerated in the prison. Pizarro, having posted a sentry and a trumpeter on the battlements to give warning of the minister's arrival, bribes Rocco to help him dispose of the prisoner, who is indeed Florestan, held in solitary confinement in the deepest dungeon. Rocco is to dig a grave, while Pizarro himself will kill his enemy. Leonore, who has overheard part of this conversation, expresses her feelings of outrage, and then learns from Rocco of the governor's permission for the marriage and for Fidelio to help dig the grave for the unknown prisoner. Meanwhile, the less dangerous political prisoners on the upper levels have been let out into the courtyard and sing, with cautious ecstasy, of their joy at seeing the sun and breathing fresh air. Pizarro storms in, demanding to know why the prisoners have been let out of their cells. Rocco offers the King's saint's day as an ostensible excuse, but Pizarro orders them back into their cells as Rocco and Fidelio prepare to descend to the lowest dungeon.

ACT 2. In his cell, Florestan (tenor), in chains and deprived of light, heat, and nourishment, prays that his ordeal may soon be over. He imagines he sees his wife Leonore before him, then collapses senseless. Rocco and Fidelio arrive and unblock the old cistern to make a grave. When Florestan wakes from his trance, Leonore recognizes him as her husband. She begs to be allowed to give the prisoner some wine and a stale crust of bread, which Rocco reluctantly allows. The jailer gives the signal to Pizarro that all is prepared, and after dismissing Fidelio, the governor reveals his identity to Florestan. He is about to stab him with a dagger when Fidelio, who has been in hiding in the darkness, rushes forward. Proclaiming that she is Florestan's wife, and drawing a pistol, she interposes herself between Pizarro and his victim. At that moment the trumpet call announcing the arrival of the minister from Seville is heard, followed by Jacquino's excited confirmation. Rocco calls for torches to light the governor up the steps, and Leonore and Florestan fall into each other's arms.

Outside the prison, Don Fernando (bass), the minister, addresses the released prisoners and their relatives. When Rocco appears with Florestan and Leonore, Fernando, though overjoyed that his friend is still alive, expresses horror and amazement that he is in chains. Pizarro's excuses are cut short, and the governor is arrested by his own guard. Leonore is given the key with which to unlock her husband's fetters, and after a prayer of thanks to God, the crowd, led by Florestan, jubilantly hails the courage of a wife willing to risk her life for her husband.

The earlier version of the opera, which ends on a more ambivalent, less positively joyful note than the 1814 version, is sometimes performed today under the title of *Leonore*.

Bellini, Vincenzo (1801–36), Italian composer. After two previous attempts—a student piece, *Adelson e Salvini* (1825), and a commission for Naples, *Bianca e Gernando* (1826)—Bellini scored a major success with his third opera, *Il pirata* (The Pirate), which was produced at La Scala, Milan in 1827. This opera already displayed the Sicilian-born composer's particular gift for long, seemingly endless melodies. *La straniera* (The Foreign Woman), which followed at La Scala two years later, was not so much liked, nor was *Zaira*, produced at Parma in 1829. But *I Capuleti e i Montecchi*, based on Shakespeare's *Romeo and Juliet*, and first produced at Venice in 1830, immediately became popular. *La sonnambula* and *Norma*, Bellini's best-known and, in their different ways, most typical operas, both date from 1831 and form the peak of an all-too-brief career. *Beatrice di Tenda*, produced at Venice in 1833, was less popular. *I puritani* (The Puritans) began a triumphant progress in Paris during January 1835; eight months later the composer died at Puteaux, just outside the French capital.

La sonnambula (The Sleep-walker), opera in two acts, with text by Felice Romani, first produced on 6 March 1831 at the Teatro Carcano, Milan. Set in a village in Switzerland, early in the nineteenth century.

ACT 1. Amina (soprano), foster-daughter to Teresa

(mezzo-soprano), who owns the mill, is betrothed to Elvino (tenor), a young farmer. The entire village celebrates the betrothal ceremony, apart from Lisa (soprano), proprietress of the inn, who is herself in love with Elvino. After the contract is signed and Elvino has presented Amina with a ring, the festivities are interrupted by the arrival of a stranger in officer's uniform. It is Count Rodolfo (bass), owner of the castle overlooking the village, returning home after many years' absence, and at first unrecognized by the villagers. He compliments the bride on her beauty, arousing jealousy in Elvino's heart. Warned of a phantom that has been haunting the village, Rodolfo decides to spend the night at the inn, more drawn by Lisa's attractions than he is afraid of the ghost.

Rodolfo is shown to his bedchamber by Lisa, who informs him that his identity is now known, and that the villagers are coming to welcome him later that night. The Count and Lisa are enjoying a flirtation when a noise is heard outside his window. Lisa hides in the adjoining room, and Rodolfo is amazed to see Amina, dressed in white, enter his room through the window. He realizes not only that Amina is sleepwalking but also that she is obviously the 'phantom'. Not wishing to awaken or embarrass her, Rodolfo blows out his candle and leaves the room as Amina lies down on the bed. The villagers arrive to welcome the Count. Seeing a woman on the bed, they are about to creep away when Lisa enters with a light and shows Elvino the sleeping Amina. Abruptly woken, confused and unable to explain how she came to be there, Amina is furiously accused of betrayal by Elvino. No one believes in her innocence except for Teresa, who wraps a scarf hanging on the bedpost round her foster-daughter's neck and leads her away.

ACT 2. Amina meets Elvino on the pathway leading

up to the castle, where the villagers have gone to ask the Count to intercede on behalf of Amina with the young man. Although Amina again protests her innocence, Elvino rejects her, tearing his betrothal ring from her finger.

The villagers are again about to celebrate a wedding, this time between Lisa and Elvino. Rodolfo tries to explain that Amina was walking in her sleep, but Elvino, who has never heard of sleepwalking, refuses to believe him. Teresa implores the villagers to celebrate more quietly, as Amina is asleep in the mill. When Teresa discovers that Lisa intends to marry Elvino, she produces the scarf which she found on the bedpost in the Count's bedroom, having recognized it as the innkeeper's property. Elvino is partly convinced of Amina's innocence. Just then Amina emerges in her nightdress from the window of her bedroom in the mill, and walks across the narrow bridge spanning the mill-wheel. Transfixed, the villagers pray for her safety and, despite a rotten plank that breaks under her foot, Amina reaches the other side of the stream, and kneels to pray for Elvino. Totally convinced at last, he replaces his ring on her finger. Amina awakes to find her beloved kneeling before her, and the delighted villagers singing her praises.

Norma, opera in two acts, with text by Felice Romani, based on a tragedy by L. A. Soumet. First performed on 26 December 1831 at La Scala, Milan. Set in Gaul during the Roman occupation, about 50 BC.

ACT 1. Norma (soprano), high priestess of the Druidical temple, has fallen in love with Pollione (tenor), the Roman pro-consul, and has secretly borne him two children.

The Druids, led by Oroveso (bass), Archdruid and father to Norma, come to the sacred grove to pray for strength to throw off the Roman yoke. When they have gone, Pollione confesses to Flavio (tenor), his centurion, that he no longer loves Norma but has become enamoured of Adalgisa (soprano), a temple virgin, whom he plans to abduct and take back with him to Rome. At the sound of the sacred gong the Romans leave, as Druids and priestesses gather in the grove. Norma, afraid for the safety of Pollione, whom she still loves, tries to damp the ardour of the warlike Druids by prophesying that Rome will fall of its own volition. Mounting the Druidical stone, she cuts a sprig of mistletoe from the branches of the oak of Irminsul. She prays to the chaste goddess of the moon to bring peace, finally promising the Gauls that when the hour for rebellion does strike, she will summon them to war.

After everyone has gone, Adalgisa remains behind to pray for protection from Irminsul. Pollione finds her there and urges her to go with him to Rome. After much hesitation, she agrees.

In Norma's dwelling, the priestess embraces her children and tells Clotilde (soprano), her confidante, to hide them, as she hears someone coming. It is Adalgisa, who unburdens her heart to Norma without, however, naming the Roman she loves. At the entrance of Pollione, Norma realizes the identity of Adalgisa's would-be abductor, and launches into a furious tirade against him. Adalgisa sides with Norma against Pollione, and the act ends with a magnificent trio.

ACT 2. Norma contemplates killing her two sleeping children, as the offspring of the infamous Pollione; but she cannot do it and, calling for Clotilde, asks her to fetch Adalgisa. When the latter arrives, Norma announces that she will kill herself, and begs Adalgisa to take the children to Pollione in the Roman camp. Adalgisa refuses; she cannot love a man who has behaved so treacherously to another woman. The two women affirm their affection for each other.

The Druids are told by Oroveso that the time for rebellion is not yet; they must wait patiently. In the temple of Irminsul, Norma awaits Adalgisa, who has gone to urge Pollione to return to Norma and their children. When Clotilde reports that Pollione has refused Adalgisa's pleading, and has vowed to abduct her, Norma again becomes furiously angry and, striking the gong three times, summons the Druids and warriors of Gaul to war. Pollione, who has been caught violating the cloister of the virgins, is dragged in, and Norma announces that he will be the sacrificial victim. She raises her dagger but is unable to kill Pollione in cold blood, and requests that they be left alone together. Norma demands that Pollione swear to abandon Adalgisa. He refuses, but offers to kill himself if Norma will spare Adalgisa. Norma also refuses, and threatens all of them—Pollione, his children and Adalgisa will perish if he does not renounce the young priestess.

The Druids return and Norma announces that she has changed her mind; the sacrificial victim will be a priestess who has broken her vows—herself. Oroveso and the people are at first incredulous, then hostile. Pollione finds his love for Norma returning. When Norma mounts the funeral pyre, having implored Oroveso to spare her children, Pollione accompanies her.

I puritani (The Puritans), opera in three acts, with text by Carlo Pepoli, based on the historical drama *Têtes rondes et cavaliers* by J. A. Ancelot and J. X. B. Saintine. First performed on 24 January 1835 at the Théâtre-Italien, Paris. Set in Plymouth during the English Civil War, *I puritani* derives at several removes from two novels by Sir Walter Scott, *The Covenanters* and *Old Mortality*, hence its full title *I puritani di Scozia*—the Scottish Puritans.

Berg, Alban (1885–1935), Austrian composer. Although greatly influenced by his teacher, Schoenberg, Berg adopted the older composer's 12-tone system only for his second opera, *Lulu*. In the first, *Wozzeck*, he used a different musical form for each of the 15 short scenes. *Lulu* was left unfinished at Berg's death. After initial attempts to find a composer willing to complete the work had failed—one of those approached was Schoenberg—Berg's widow refused to allow anyone to complete the opera. Consequently, *Lulu* was given in truncated form until after the death of Frau Berg in 1976, when the orchestration of Act 3, for which the composer had left fairly elaborate sketches, was completed by Friedrich Cerha.

Wozzeck, opera in three acts, with text adapted by the composer from the drama *Woyzeck* by Georg Büchner. First performed on 14 December 1925 at the Berlin State Opera. It is set in a garrison town in the 1830s.

ACT 1. The Captain (tenor) is being shaved by his batman, Wozzeck (baritone), and observes that his servant, though a good fellow, has no sense of morality, as he has fathered a child out of wedlock. Wozzeck replies that morality is for the rich, not for poor men like himself.

Wozzeck and his fellow soldier Andres (tenor) are cutting sticks at sunset outside the town. Wozzeck imagines the place to be haunted, and believes the whole world is on fire.

Marie (soprano), the mother of Wozzeck's child, is looking out of the window of her room, listening to a military band. She watches the Drum-major (tenor), who waves to her. After a slanging match with her neighbour, Margret (mezzo-soprano), Marie sings a cradle song to her child. Wozzeck knocks on the window, but is in too much of a hurry to come in, or even to look at the child.

The Doctor (bass), who is using Wozzeck as a guinea-pig for his experiments, complains that the latter does not follow his instructions as to diet, etc, closely enough, and confuses him still further with scientific theories that will one day bring the Doctor fame.

In the street outside Marie's house the Drum-major is showing off his uniform and bragging about his Sunday get-up, which is even finer. Marie repulses his advances once, then succumbs and leads him inside the house.

ACT 2. Marie is trying on some earrings that the Drum-major has given her, and admiring herself in a broken mirror. When Wozzeck comes in, she explains that she has found the earrings but he does not believe her. He gives her money earned from the Captain and the Doctor and, after a look at the sleeping child, leaves. Marie is ashamed of her infidelity.

The Doctor, stopped by the Captain in the street, warns his friend that he may have an apoplectic fit at any moment. When Wozzeck appears, they taunt him in veiled but unmistakable terms about Marie's affair with the Drum-major.

Marie is standing in the street outside her house. Wozzeck accuses her of being as beautiful as sin, and seems about to strike her. 'Better a knife-blade in the heart than lay a hand on me', she warns. Wozzeck repeats her words as he hurries away.

In a beer-garden, workmen and soldiers are dancing with their girls to a band on stage. Wozzeck jealously watches as the Drum-major and Marie dance together. Andres and the soldiers sing a song, and a drunken workman (baritone) holds a confused discourse. A Simpleton (tenor) remarks to Wozzeck that the scene is joyful but reeks of blood.

Snores are heard from the sleeping soldiers in the barracks. Wozzeck cannot sleep because of images from the scene in the beer-garden. The Drum-major, staggering in drunkenly, boasts of his conquest of Marie. He provokes a fight with Wozzeck, leaving him bruised and bleeding on the floor.

ACT 3. In her room at night, Marie is reading the story of Mary Magdalen from her Bible. She compares her own behaviour with that of the Magdalen.

Later that night, Wozzeck and Marie walk by a pond in the wood. She wishes to return home but he prevents her and, as the moon rises, cuts her throat with his knife.

Wozzeck is dancing at an inn with Margret. She notices blood on his hand and he pretends to have cut his arm, before rushing away from the other dancers' curiosity.

By the pond, Wozzeck searches for and finds the knife with which he killed Marie; he throws it into the water, then wades into the pond to wash off the blood. The Doctor and the Captain walk by. They think they hear a man drowning, but do not stop.

After an interlude in which the tragedy is re-enacted in the orchestra, the final scene takes place outside Marie's house, where children are playing, including Marie's child. Others run in to announce the discovery of Marie's murder, but her child is too young to understand and remains contentedly playing alone as they go off to see the corpse.

Lulu, opera in three acts, with text adapted by the composer from the dramas *Earth Spirit* and *Pandora's Box* by Frank Wedekind. First performed, in a two-act version, on 2 June 1937 at Zurich; in a three-act version, completed by Friedrich Cerha, on 24 February 1979 at the Paris Opéra. In the Prologue, an Animal Tamer (bass) exhibits the animals in his menagerie. The most dangerous of all, he declares, is the snake—and Lulu is brought on.

ACT 1. Lulu (soprano), married to the Medical Specialist, is having her portrait painted in pierrot costume, watched by Dr Schön (baritone), an editor who is Lulu's adoptive father and lover. Schön's son Alwa (tenor), a composer, arrives to fetch his father. Left alone with Lulu, the Painter (tenor) declares his passionate love for her. The Medical Specialist, arriving in the middle of a seduction scene, has a heart attack and dies.

Lulu, now married to the Painter, and living in a luxury owed chiefly to Dr Schön's patronage of her husband, learns of Schön's engagement to a respectable young woman. The Painter goes to his studio just as Schigolch (bass), whom he takes to be a beggar, arrives. Schigolch is an old lover of Lulu's, believed to be her father by Dr Schön, who interrupts their companiable chat together. Schön tells Lulu that their relationship must end; he wishes to be free to marry, but she will not let him go. Their quarrel disturbs the Painter, to whom Schön now reveals the truth of Lulu's past. The Painter goes to speak to Lulu, or so he says, as Alwa comes in. Hearing a noise in the next room, father and son break down the door to find that the Painter has committed suicide.

Lulu is appearing as a dancer in Alwa's latest show. In her dressing-room she talks to Alwa as she changes her costume, then goes on stage. His consideration of whether her story might do as the basis of an opera is interrupted by the arrival of the Prince (tenor), a traveller who wishes to marry Lulu and take her with him to Africa. Lulu returns in a state of hysteria. She has seen Dr Schön in a box with his fiancée, and refuses to continue her performance. She forces Schön, when they are left alone together, to admit that his subjugation to her is as complete as before, then dictates a letter in which he breaks off his engagement.

ACT 2. Lulu, now married to Dr Schön, is entertaining her admirers, who include Countess Geschwitz (mezzo-soprano), a Lesbian painter, Schigolch, Rodrigo (bass), an Acrobat, and a Schoolboy (contralto). Alwa is announced, and the other visitors hide in various parts of the room. Dr Schön, who had earlier gone off to the stock exchange, returns to hear his son make a passionate declaration of love to Lulu. Becoming aware of the other, hidden admirers, Schön threatens the Acrobat with a revolver, then gives it to Lulu, trying to make her kill herself. Instead, she shoots him in the back while his attention is distracted by the Schoolboy. As Schön dies, he blames Geschwitz. Alwa calls the police and Lulu is arrested, despite her offer to Alwa of eternal devotion.

An orchestral interlude—in some productions illustrated by a silent-film sequence—describes the ensuing events. Lulu is tried for the murder of Dr Schön, found guilty, and condemned to prison. Countess Geschwitz makes use of an outbreak of cholera to devise an elaborate plan of escape in which Lulu is infected with cholera, and transferred to an isolation hospital.

In Dr Schön's house, Geschwitz waits for Schigolch, who is to take her to the hospital where she will change places with Lulu, completing the plan of escape. The Acrobat, who is being bribed to take Lulu as partner in his circus act, is appalled by her appearance when she arrives, dressed in Geschwitz's clothes, and threatens to call the police. Alwa again protests his love for Lulu, brushing aside her claim to have killed his mother, and her observation that his father bled to death on the very sofa on which they are sitting.

ACT 3. Lulu, Alwa, Geschwitz and the Acrobat have escaped to Paris. In the salon of a casino, the Marquis (tenor) is blackmailing Lulu. He threatens to inform on her to the police unless she agrees to work for him in a

Cairo brothel or pay him a large sum of money. The Acrobat also blackmails Lulu for more money; and Schigolch requires cash to support his new mistress. As the gamblers bewail their losses—the Banker (bass) has won everything—and the collapse of the Jungfrau Railway shares in which they have all invested, Lulu arranges for Geschwitz to lure the Acrobat to Schigolch's room, where the latter will dispose of him. Then Lulu, after changing clothes with the Page (contralto), escapes with Alwa as the police, summoned by the Marquis, arrive to re-arrest her.

In London, Lulu resorts to prostitution to support herself, Alwa and Schigolch. Her first client is a Professor (mute role, the same actor as Lulu's first husband, the Medical Specialist). Geschwitz now arrives with Lulu's pierrot portrait, which has accompanied her on all the stages of her spectacular rise and fall. Lulu's second client, the Negro (tenor, the same singer as her second husband, the Painter), refuses to pay and kills Alwa when he tries to intervene. Lulu's third client, Jack the Ripper (baritone, the same singer as her third husband, Dr Schön), kills first Lulu and then Geschwitz, who tries to save her.

Berkeley, (Sir) Lennox (born 1903), English composer. His first opera, *Nelson* (1953), was produced at Sadler's Wells without much success. His second, the one-act comedy *A Dinner Engagement*, fared better. Its first production at Aldeburgh (1954) was followed by many other stagings in Britain. Neither *Ruth* (1956) nor *The Castaway* (1967) repeated that success.

Berlioz, Hector (1803–69), French composer. It was not until the second half of the twentieth century that Berlioz received full recognition as a powerful and highly individual operatic composer. *Benvenuto Cellini* was a failure on its first performance in Paris (1838) and an even worse flop in London 15 years later. *Les Troyens* (The Trojans), his two-part adaptation of Virgil's *Aeneid*, was never performed complete in the composer's lifetime. *Béatrice et Bénédict*, based on Shakespeare's *Much Ado about Nothing*, was not staged in France until after the composer's death, either, although it had been performed in Germany in 1863. *La Damnation de Faust*, a 'dramatic legend' not originally intended for the theatre, was for a century the dramatic work by Berlioz best-known to audiences both in France and outside it.

Benvenuto Cellini, opera in three acts (originally two), with text by Léon de Wailly and August Barbier, based on Cellini's autobiography. First produced on 10 September 1838 at the Paris Opéra. Set in Rome at the end of Carnival, 1532, the opera deals with the Florentine goldsmith's completion of a statue of Perseus commissioned by Pope Clement VII.

La Damnation de Faust, dramatic legend in four parts, with text adapted by the composer from Gérard de Nerval's version of Goethe's play. First performed (in concert) on 6 December 1846 at the Opéra-Comique, Paris. First staged on 18 February 1893 at Monte Carlo Opera House.

PART 1 takes place on the plains of Hungary. Faust (tenor) sings of the beauties of nature, peasants sing and dance, and soldiers march by to the Rákóczi March.

PART 2. Faust is in his study, about to drink poison and end his joyless existence. The sound of the Easter Hymn, 'Christ is Risen', gives him new hope. Then Mephistopheles (bass) appears, offering to provide Faust with all the joy he desires.

The revelry of students and soldiers in Auerbach's cellar in Leipzig does not please Faust, but a vision of Marguerite (soprano) impresses him with her beauty.

PART 3. Faust is brought by Mephistopheles to

Marguerite's bedroom. He hides as she enters; after singing the ballad of the King of Thule, she lies down to sleep. There follows the Minuet of the Will-o-the-wisps, and Mephistopheles' mocking Serenade. Faust awakens Marguerite and the two sing a passionate love duet, which is turned into a trio as Mephistopheles warns Faust to leave before his presence is discovered.

PART 4. Marguerite, deserted by Faust, sings sadly of her lost love. In a mountain gorge Faust again invokes the beauties of nature. Hearing from Mephistopheles that Marguerite is in prison for poisoning her mother with a sleeping draught, Faust signs away his soul in an attempt to save her. But after the Ride to the Abyss, Faust is carried off by demons to Hell. Angelic voices announce the apotheosis of Marguerite, and welcome her into Heaven.

Les Troyens (The Trojans), opera in five acts, with text by the composer after Virgil's *Aeneid*, usually divided into two parts: *La Prise de Troie* (The Capture of Troy), first performed on 6 December 1890 at Karlsruhe; and *Les Troyens à Carthage* (The Trojans in Carthage), first performed on 4 November 1863 at the Théâtre-Lyrique, Paris. The complete work was first produced on 6 and 7 December 1890 at Karlsruhe.

The Capture of Troy

ACT 1. Outside the city, the people of Troy rejoice that the long war against the Greeks is over. Cassandra (soprano), daughter of King Priam (bass), prophesies the fall of Troy but nobody, not even her lover Choroebus (baritone), believes her. The Wooden Horse, left behind by the Greeks, is dragged triumphantly into the city after Aeneas (tenor) has described the death of Laocoon, the Trojan priest. The priest has been devoured by two serpents from the sea, presumably as a punishment for suspecting the Horse, which is dedicated to the goddess Pallas.

ACT 2. Aeneas lies asleep in his palace. He is woken by the Ghost of Hector (bass), who tells him that Troy has fallen after being infiltrated by the Greek soldiers hidden in the Horse. Priam is dead. Aeneas and his son Ascanius (mezzo-soprano) are to take ship to Italy, and there found a new Troy. In the Temple of Vesta, Cassandra and the other women of Troy kill themselves rather than be captured by the Greeks. They are inspired by the knowledge that Aeneas has escaped.

The Trojans in Carthage

ACT 3. Dido, Queen of Carthage (mezzo-soprano), receives homage and tributes from her people, but confesses privately to her sister Anna (contralto) that her heart is strangely troubled. Anna suggests that Dido has been lonely since the death of her husband, and needs a new one, just as Carthage needs a new king. Iopas (tenor), a Carthaginian poet, announces the arrival of a band of foreigners whose ships have been driven ashore in a storm. Dido welcomes them and, to the strains of the Trojan March (now in the minor), Aeneas and his men, disguised as sailors, are led in by Ascanius. When Narbal (bass), Dido's minister, arrives with the news that Carthage has been attacked by Numidian troops, Aeneas throws off his disguise and offers to lead his own men and Dido's army against the invaders.

ACT 4. The victory of Aeneas over the Numidians is celebrated in the palace garden. Anna thinks that the Trojan hero would make a splendid husband for Dido, and king for Carthage, but Narbal is aware that Aeneas' destiny will lead him away from Carthage to Italy. After dances and a song by Iopas have failed to hold the attention of Dido, she begs Aeneas to relate once again the tale of the fall of Troy, especially the marriage of Andromache, the widow of Hector, to Pyrrhus, son of Hector's murderer Achilles. Left alone, Dido and Aeneas express their mutual love, but the word 'Italy' on the lips of a statue of Mercury warns Aeneas that his destiny must be fulfilled. During the Royal Hunt and Storm, a symphonic interlude, Dido and Aeneas shelter from the storm in a cave, and consummate their love.

ACT 5. By the harbour, where the Trojan ships lie at anchor, Aeneas, though passionately in love with Dido and aware of the pain his departure will cause her, decides that he can no longer put off his destiny. The Queen pleads with him to stay but he is adamant and, to the sound of the March, boards his ship. When Iopas describes to Dido the sailing of the Trojan fleet, she orders a funeral pyre to be lit, and everything left behind by Aeneas to be placed on it. She says farewell to the city of Carthage, then, escorted by Anna and Narbal, mounts the funeral pyre and kills herself with Aeneas' sword. The Carthaginians curse the Trojans but, as Dido dies, she sees a vision of Rome, the eternal city that Aeneas will found in Italy.

Bizet, Georges (1835–75), French composer. Bizet began his career auspiciously by winning joint first prize (with Lecoq) in the competition set up by Offenbach for a one-act comic opera. Bizet's *Dr Miracle*, first produced at the Théâtre des Bouffes-Parisiennes in 1857, did not have its London premiere until a century later, but is now fairly frequently performed. His next two operas, *Don Procopio* (1859) and *Ivan IV* (1863), were not produced until many years after the composer's death. *Les Pêcheurs de perles* (The Pearl Fishers) scored a modest success on its production in 1863. *La Jolie fille de Perth*, an adaptation of Walter Scott's novel *The Fair Maid of Perth*, was first produced at the Théâtre-Lyrique, Paris, in December 1867, after several postponements. It received a good press but only 18 performances, the same number as *The Pearl Fishers*. In the next six years, of more than a dozen operatic projects, some scarcely

(right)
Beethoven *Fidelio*. English National Opera, 1980. Marzelline (Eilene Hannan), Leonore (Josephine Barstow) (Andrew March)

(below) Britten *A Midsummer Night's Dream*. Glyndebourne, 1981. Tytania (Ileana Cotrubas), Oberon (James Bowman) (Guy Gravett)

(*above*) Charpentier *Louise*. English National Opera, 1981. Louise (Valerie Masterson), the Father (Richard Van Allan), the Mother (Katherine Pring) (Zoë Dominic)

(*right*) Donizetti *L'elisir d'amore*. Royal Opera Covent Garden, 1976. Doctor Dulcamara (Geraint Evans) (Donald Southern)

(*above*) Donizetti *Lucia di Lammermoor*. Royal Opera Covent Garden, 1973. Lucia (Joan Sutherland), Edgardo (Luciano Pavarotti) (Donald Southern)

(*below*) Gounod *Faust*. Royal Opera Covent Garden, 1977. Faust (Alfredo Kraus), Mephistopheles (Nicolai Ghiaurov), Marguerite (Mirella Freni) (Donald Southern)

(*above*) Henze *We come to the River*. Royal Opera Covent Garden, 1976. The General (Norman Welsby) and Mad People (Donald Southern)

(*right*) Janáček *Jenufa*. Deutsche Oper, Berlin, 1976. The Kostelnicka (Patricia Johnson) (Ilse Buhs)

begun, some half-finished, only the one-act *Djamileh* was performed, at the Opéra-Comique, in 1872. Bizet spent the next two years composing his masterpiece, *Carmen*. This was first heard three months before the composer's premature death, which the poor reception accorded to the opera is popularly supposed to have hastened. *Carmen*, for many decades one of the best-loved operas ever written, started on its triumphal path in October 1875 with a production in Vienna, for which Guiraud supplied sung recitatives to replace the spoken dialogue. It was not until comparatively recently that the original version gained currency once more.

Les Pêcheurs de perles, opera in three acts, with text by M. Carré and E. Cormon. First performed on 30 September 1863 at the Théâtre-Lyrique, Paris. The opera is set in Ceylon.

ACT 1. The pearl fishermen are choosing a chief. Zurga (baritone) is selected. He welcomes Nadir (tenor), who is returning to the village after a long absence. Once rivals for the love of the priestess Leila, they have nevertheless sworn an oath of friendship. The high priest, Nourabad (bass), brings the veiled virgin who is to protect the fishermen with her prayers while they are at sea. She is welcomed by Zurga and the fishermen, but Nadir recognizes her as Leila (soprano), whom he still loves. Leila sings an invocation to Brahma, then takes her position on the rock where she will keep her vigil.

ACT 2. Nourabad warns Leila she will be killed if she betrays her vow. Left alone, Leila sings of her love for Nadir, whom she has recognized. His voice is heard serenading her, then he arrives and the two sing of their mutual love. When Nadir leaves, he is seen by Nourabad, who sends the temple guards to capture him. Zurga, as chief, claims the right to judge Nadir himself, meaning to save his friend from the anger of the priests and fishermen, but when Nourabad tears off Leila's veil and Zurga recognizes her, he swears to be revenged on Nadir.

ACT 3. Leila comes to plead with Zurga in his tent for the life of Nadir; she will gladly die in his place. Zurga, overcome by jealousy, refuses and Leila leaves, giving him a necklace she would like sent to her mother. Meanwhile a funeral pyre has been built on the shore. Just as Leila and Nadir are about to be sacrificed, Zurga brings news that the camp is on fire and the fishermen run to fight the flames, which are visible in the distance. Zurga frees Leila and Nadir, telling them that he himself had started the fire. He had recognized Leila's necklace as one he had given to an unknown girl who once saved his life. The lovers escape, while Zurga stays behind to prevent pursuit. He is denounced by Nourabad and stabbed to death.

Carmen, opera in four acts with text by H. Meilhac and L. Halévy, based on the novel by Prosper Merimée. First performed on 3 March 1875 at the Opéra-Comique, Paris. The action takes place in Seville, about 1820.

ACT 1. Outside the cigarette factory a crowd is waiting to see the guard changed. Morales (baritone) and other dragoons in the out-going guard waylay Micaela (soprano), a pretty young peasant girl. She is looking for Don José (tenor), Corporal of Dragoons who, the others tell her, will shortly be arriving with the relief guard. Micaela leaves, saying she will return, as the new guard, preceded by a band of urchins and headed by Captain Zuniga (bass) and José, marches in. José recognizes Micaela from Morales' description, but just then the factory bell rings, summoning the girls back to work. They drift in with their admirers, and last of all comes Carmen (mezzo-soprano), a gypsy. She sings a habanera to an admiring crowd; only Don José pays no attention, so it is to him that she throws a red cassia-flower from her corsage before running into the factory. José picks it up and conceals it inside his tunic as Micaela returns. She has brought him a letter and some money from his mother, and also a kiss, which she shyly delivers on his forehead, before leaving him to read the letter. José decides to forget the fascinating gypsy and marry Micaela, as his mother suggests. A tremendous row breaks out in the cigarette factory; the girls run out screaming that Carmen has attacked another girl with a knife, and Zuniga sends José and two dragoons to arrest her. Carmen will not answer the Captain's questions, except with 'Tra, la, la', so Zuniga goes to write an order committing her to prison. Left alone with Don José, Carmen sings a seguidilla, promising to love him and to meet him at Lillas Pastia's tavern if he lets her escape. José resists at first, but cannot hold out against her attraction, and loosens the rope binding her wrists. Zuniga returns with the prison-order; José and two dragoons escort Carmen, who throws away the rope, pushes her guards and escapes into the crowd, which hinders the soldiers from pursuing her. José is arrested.

ACT 2. In Lillas Pastia's tavern, Carmen and her friends Frasquita and Mercedes (sopranos) entertain Zuniga and Morales. A procession, headed by the toreador Escamillo (baritone), enters the tavern. Escamillo sings his famous Toreador's song, then leaves, taking the officers with him. The three girls are joined by two smugglers, Dancairo (tenor) and Remendado (baritone), who want to leave right away, but Carmen refuses. She is in love with José, who went to prison in her place, and has been released that day. José's voice is heard outside the tavern. The smugglers go into another room, advising Carmen to recruit her dragoon into their band. After a rapturous reunion, Carmen dances for José as, she tells him, she danced for his officers. He is jealous but, when the bugle sounding the retreat is heard, announces that he must return to barracks. Carmen is furious and accuses him of not loving her. In answer he pulls from his pocket the flower, now crushed and faded, that she had thrown him. Carmen is mollified, but insists that if he really loved her he would stay and join the smugglers' band. José refuses but, when Zuniga returns looking for Carmen, he draws his sabre, and the two men fight. The smugglers rush in, disarm Zuniga and take him away. José has no option but to join the band.

ACT 3. The smugglers arrive in a rocky pass in the mountains with their contraband, and rest while Dancairo and Remendado go off to reconnoitre. Carmen has already tired of José, who is not suited to the smugglers' life, but he is passionately jealous and refuses to leave her. Frasquita and Mercedes tell their fortunes with the cards. Carmen also produces a pack of cards; her destiny is death, a fate she will not try to evade. Dancairo and Remendado return with news that the border guards are susceptible to the charms of Carmen and the other girls. The smugglers depart down the gorge, leaving José as look-out. He climbs up a rock, and Micaela, who has come to find José, enters the camp. Though frightened, she is determined to reclaim him. A shot is heard, and she hides as José descends from his look-out post. The intruder is Escamillo who, he tells José, has come to see Carmen, having heard that she has tired of her present lover, the ex-dragoon. José discloses his identity, and the two men draw knives to fight. They are separated by the returning smugglers, and Escamillo pays elaborate court to Carmen, inviting her and her friends to his next bullfight in Seville. Micaela is discovered, and at first José refuses to accompany her. When she tells him that his mother is dying, he agrees. After warning Carmen that they will meet again, José sets off with Micaela, as the voice of Escamillo is heard in a mocking refrain of the Toreador's song.

ACT 4. Outside the bull-ring in Seville, the crowds wait for the toreadors. Escamillo arrives escorting Carmen and, after declaring his love for her, enters the arena. Frasquita and Mercedes warn Carmen that José has been seen in the neighbourhood. She is not afraid, and waits to confront him as the crowd pours into the arena. José, his clothes dirty and torn, begs her to return to him, for he still loves her. She proudly refuses and, as shouts of 'Escamillo!' are heard from the arena, tries to go inside. José intercepts her and kills her with a knife. As the crowd emerges from the arena, the guards arrest José, who offers no resistance.

Bliss, (Sir) Arthur (1891–1975), English composer. His opera *The Olympians*, with text by J. B. Priestley, was produced at Covent Garden in 1949. A later work, *Tobias and the Angel*, with text by Christopher Hassall, was conceived as a television opera and shown on BBC television in 1960. It was later adapted for the theatre.

Blomdahl, Karl-Birger (1916–68), Swedish composer. His space-opera, *Aniara*, was produced at the Royal Opera, Stockholm, in May 1959. It was seen in Edinburgh later the same year, and at Covent Garden in 1960. A spaceship is carrying refugees to Mars from an Earth devastated by atomic warfare. It collides with an asteroid and, knocked off course, is doomed to fly for ever through space.

Blow, John (1649–1708), English composer. Blow's only opera, *Venus and Adonis*, was devised as a court entertainment for Charles II. It was first performed in

London about 1684, with Mary Davies, the King's mistress, as Venus, and Mary Tudor, her daughter by Charles, as Cupid.

Boieldieu, Adrien (1775–1834), French composer. He wrote more than 30 operas, and also collaborated on several others. His works were extremely popular in Paris, and the best-known are probably *Ma Tante Aurore*, produced at the Opéra-Comique in 1803; *Jean de Paris*, staged at the same theatre in 1812; and Boieldieu's masterpiece, *La Dame blanche* (The White Lady), with text by Eugène Scribe based on Walter Scott's novels *The Monastery* and *Guy Mannering*. This opera received nearly 2,000 performances at the Opéra-Comique in the century following its premiere in 1825.

Boito, Arrigo (1842–1918), Italian composer and librettist. Probably best known today for the texts he adapted from Shakespeare for Verdi's last two operas, *Otello* and *Falstaff*, Boito also composed two operas. *Mefistofele*, based on Goethe's *Faust*, was first produced at La Scala, Milan, in 1868. It was withdrawn after two performances during which the audiences had displayed their hostility in no uncertain terms. (*Mefistofele*, cut and considerably revised, was successfully produced in 1875 at Bologna.) *Nerone* (Nero) was left unfinished at his death, although Boito had been working on the text and music for over 50 years. Toscanini conducted the first performance in 1924 at La Scala.

Borodin, Alexander (1833–87), Russian composer. Apart from *The Bogatirs* (1867), a pastiche incorporating music by Rossini, Meyerbeer, Offenbach and others, as well as original material, Borodin finished none of the four operas that he began to compose. *The Tsar's Bride* was re-used in other works, and *Mlada* (Borodin was contributing only one act) remained incomplete and unperformed. But *Prince Igor*, on which Borodin had been working for 18 years when he died, was completed by Rimsky-Korsakov and Glazounov, and first produced in 1890 at the Maryinsky Theatre, St Petersburg. Prince Igor (baritone) and his son Vladimir (tenor) are captured by the Polovtsian Khan Kontchak (bass), who entertains his noble captives with barbaric dances. Meanwhile Igor's wife Yaroslavna (soprano) is left in the care of her profligate brother, Prince Galitsky (bass). Igor eventually escapes to be reunited with his wife, but Vladimir remains behind to marry Kontchakovna (mezzo-soprano), the Khan's daughter.

Britten, Benjamin (Lord Britten of Aldeburgh) (1913–76), English composer. Britten's first opera, *Paul Bunyan*, with a text by W. H. Auden, was produced in 1941 at Columbia University, New York, and then withdrawn by the composer. In a revised version it was given at the 1976 Aldeburgh Festival. The success of *Peter Grimes*, with which Sadler's Wells re-opened after World War II, seemed to herald a new chapter in the history of British opera. But Britten temporarily abandoned large-scale opera: *The Rape of Lucretia* (1946), *Albert Herring* (1947), *The Beggar's Opera* (1948), a version of Gay's ballad opera, and *Let's Make an Opera* (1949), a piece mainly for children, incorporating the opera *The Little Sweep*, were all scored for chamber orchestra or small instrumental groups. With *Billy Budd* (1951) and *Gloriana* (1953), his ill-fated contribution to the coronation of Queen Elizabeth II, Britten returned to large-scale opera, before going back to the more intimate format with *The Turn of the Screw* (1954), *Noyes Fludde* (1958), another work mainly for children, and *A Midsummer Night's Dream* (1961), an adaptation of Shakespeare's play that can be performed in either small or large theatres, though its use of boys' voices makes it more suitable for the former. Britten's three Church Parables, *Curlew River* (1964), *The Burning Fiery Furnace* (1966) and *The Prodigal Son* (1968), use economical means and original techniques derived from the Japanese Noh play to create an extremely effective form of music drama. *Owen Wingrave*, its text by Myfanwy Piper based on a story by Henry James, was originally commissioned by the BBC. It was televised in 1971 and staged at Covent Garden two years later. Britten's last opera, *Death in Venice* (1973), draws on the Church Parables and television opera in its freedom from conventional operatic forms.

Peter Grimes, opera in three acts with text by Montagu Slater, based on Crabbe's poem, *The Borough*. First performed on 7 June 1945 at Sadler's Wells Theatre, London. Set in Aldeburgh, Suffolk, about 1830.

PROLOGUE. In the Moot Hall, the inquest on Peter Grimes's boy-apprentice, who died at sea, is conducted by Swallow (bass), the coroner. The verdict is death in accidental circumstances. Grimes (tenor) fears that this will not stop the village gossips but he is reassured by Ellen Orford (soprano), the widowed schoolmistress, that they can build a new and better life for Peter.

ACT 1. The fishermen mend their nets on the beach as the village wives go about their errands. Grimes is heard calling for help to beach his boat, but no one will help him except Balstrode (baritone), a retired sea captain, and Ned Keene (baritone), the apothecary, who tells Grimes he has found him another apprentice. Hobson (bass), the carrier, refuses to collect the boy from the workhouse until Ellen offers to accompany him. A storm breaks out, and the fishermen look to the security of their boats. Balstrode asks Grimes why he does not leave the Borough and sail in a merchantman, but Grimes is 'native-rooted' in the Suffolk coast.

The storm continues in the orchestral interlude between scenes. That evening in the Boar, the pub presided over by Auntie (contralto), Balstrode and the villagers await the return of Hobson and his cart. Part of the cliff, it is rumoured, has been washed away. Mrs Sedley (mezzo-soprano), the widow of an Indian nabob, asks Keene for her pills but they, too, are arriving with the carrier. Bob Boles (tenor), the local Methodist preacher, makes drunken advances to one of Auntie's two Nieces (sopranos), the main attractions of the Boar. Grimes enters and behaves so strangely that Mrs Sedley faints. At Auntie's instigation, Ned Keene starts a round, 'Old Joe has gone fishing'. Hobson and his passengers arrive, soaked through, but Grimes insists on taking the new apprentice off to his hut immediately.

ACT 2. It is Sunday, and morning service, conducted by the rector, Horace Adams (tenor), can be heard from inside the parish church. Ellen and John, Grimes's apprentice, sit in the sun on the beach. Ellen notices that the boy has a tear in his coat and a bruise on his neck, but Grimes, who arrives to fetch the apprentice because he has seen a shoal of fish, dismisses the incident. When Ellen suggests that their plan for Grimes's rehabilitation has failed, he hits her and goes off with the boy. Mrs Sedley and Bob Boles overhear the quarrel, and soon the entire village is humming with the news that Grimes 'is at his exercise'. The men, led by Swallow, Hobson, a reluctant Balstrode and the Rector, set off for Grimes's hut to investigate, while Ellen, Auntie and the two Nieces are left to reflect on the behaviour of men.

In Grimes's hut, an upturned boat, the fisherman prepares to go to sea. Hearing the procession of villagers approaching, Grimes throws nets and tackle over the cliff and roughly encourages the boy to climb down. There is a scream as the apprentice slips and falls.

Grimes climbs quickly down himself; when the deputation arrives it finds nothing suspicious, and the Rector warns the men not to listen to their wives' gossip.

ACT 3. A dance is taking place at the Moot Hall. Swallow and Ned Keene try to detach one Niece from the other. Balstrode tells Ellen that Grimes's boat, missing for several days, is now beached, though Grimes himself is missing. She recognizes a jersey found on the tidemark as one she made for the boy, John. Mrs Sedley overhears this conversation and forces Swallow to organize a man-hunt. The villagers, succumbing to mass-hysteria, go off on their search.

A thick mist blows in from the sea as Grimes stumbles up the beach exhausted and delirious; his ramblings are accompanied only by foghorns and the distant sounds of the man-hunt. Balstrode and Ellen find Grimes, and tell him to sail out to sea and then sink his boat. With dawn the mist clears, and the fishermen return to their net-mending. A boat is reported sinking far out at sea, but the Borough continues with its daily preoccupations.

The Rape of Lucretia, opera in two acts with text by Ronald Duncan, after the play Le Viol de Lucrèce by André Obey. First produced on 12 July 1946 at Glyndebourne. The action is set in or near Rome in 500 BC.

A Male (tenor) and Female (soprano) Chorus, sitting on either side of the stage, fill in the historical background; Rome, at war with Greece, is ruled by the Etruscan prince, Tarquinius.

ACT 1. Tarquinius (baritone), Junius (bass) and Collatinus (bass), at their camp outside Rome, discuss their bet of the previous night, on the whereabouts of their wives when paid a surprise visit in Rome. Only Collatinus' wife, Lucretia, was found at home. Tarquinius and Junius quarrel, but are reconciled. After Collatinus has gone to bed, Junius, furiously jealous, puts the idea into the mind of Tarquinius of proving Lucretia's chastity.

The Male Chorus describes Tarquinius' wild ride to Rome.

At home, Lucretia (contralto), Lucia (soprano), her attendant, and Bianca (mezzo-soprano), her old nurse, have been spinning and are just about to go to bed when Tarquinius arrives, asking for hospitality for the night.

ACT 2. Lucretia lies asleep in her bedchamber. The Male Chorus describes Tarquinius' approach through the silent house. Despite Lucretia's pleading he snuffs out the candle and rapes her, an action depicted in the orchestra as the Male and Female Choruses comment on the event from an anachronistic, Christian viewpoint.

The next morning Lucia and Bianca discuss the weather, and wonder if it was Prince Tarquinius that they heard leaving the house at an early hour. Lucretia orders Lucia to send a messenger requesting Collatinus to return home at once. Bianca, troubled by her mistress's strange, hysterical mood, tries to stop the messenger, but Collatinus, accompanied by Junius, has already arrived. Lucretia, dressed in mourning, confesses to Collatinus what has happened. Then, although he offers her comfort and forgiveness, she is overcome by shame and stabs herself. After a funeral march for Lucretia, the Choruses attempt to draw a Christian moral from the story.

Albert Herring, opera in three acts, with text by Eric Crozier, after the short story by Guy de Maupassant, *Le Rosier de Madame Husson*. First performed on 20 June 1947 at Glyndebourne. Set in Loxford, a small town in East Suffolk, during April and May 1900.

ACT 1. At Lady Billows's house the committee for choosing the May Queen has been assembled. It includes Miss Wordsworth (soprano) the schoolmistress, Mr Gedge (baritone) the vicar, Mr Upfold (tenor) the mayor, Superintendent Budd (bass) and Florence Pike (contralto), Lady Billows's housekeeper. Lady Billows (soprano) opens the meeting, but none of the candidates proposed by the committee members meets with her approval. Superintendent Budd suggests a May King in the blameless person of Albert Herring from the greengrocer's. After initial outrage, Lady Billows agrees to the proposal.

In his mother's shop, Albert (tenor) is mocked by three village children, and by Sid (baritone), the butcher's assistant, and his girlfriend Nancy (mezzo-soprano) from the bakery. Florence Pike announces the arrival of Lady Billows and the committee. Albert is appalled to learn that he is to be crowned May King, but his mother Mrs Herring (mezzo-soprano) thinks of the 25 gold sovereigns he will receive.

ACT 2. May Day. In the vicarage garden a marquee has been set up, with a trestle table covered in cakes and jellies. Nancy is finishing the preparations for tea. Sid takes her outside to tell her of a scheme he has thought up, as Miss Wordsworth brings in the three children, Emmie, Cis and Harry, to rehearse their song of greeting to Albert. As they leave, Nancy and Sid return to implement the latter's scheme, which is to add rum to Albert's lemonade. The May King, now duly crowned, arrives with his procession, the children sing their piece, and everybody takes their place at table. The Vicar introduces Lady Billows, who makes a long rambling speech, and then presents Albert with his 25 gold sovereigns. The Mayor, Miss Wordsworth and Superintendent Budd add their congratulations, and Albert manages to reply 'Er, thank you—very much.'

Toasts are drunk and Albert finds the taste of his lemonade exceptionally good. It gives him hiccups, which are cured by drinking from the wrong side of his glass. Everybody attacks the tea.

Later that evening Albert returns home. He tries unsuccessfully to light the gas, then reminisces about the party—and the splendid lemonade. A whistle is heard outside; it is Sid's signal to Nancy, and Albert unwillingly hears their love duet. The thought of his totally blameless life becomes too much for him and, remembering that he has money in his pocket, he decides to go off on a spree.

ACT 3. In the shop next day, Albert's disappearance has caused general havoc. Nancy blames herself (and Sid) for spiking his lemonade. Mrs Herring is certain that her son is dead. Superintendent Budd leads the investigation, though Lady Billows would like to call in Scotland Yard. The discovery of Albert's May King wreath, crushed by a cart, appears to prove his demise. A threnody, in which each character has a verse in turn while the others lament, 'In the midst of life is death', is sung. At its climax, the shop bell rings and Albert comes in, dirty and untidy, but unhurt. Everyone but Nancy and Sid hurls abuse at him. Albert describes his night on the tiles and then politely turns the committee out of the shop; he has work to do. Even Mrs Herring is gently but firmly quelled. The mockery shown by the three children and Nancy and Sid turns to respect.

Billy Budd, opera in two acts (originally four) with text by E. M. Forster and Eric Crozier after the story by Herman Melville. First performed on 1 December 1951 at the Royal Opera House, Covent Garden. The main action takes place on board HMS *Indomitable* during 1797, framed by a prologue and epilogue in which Captain Vere (tenor), now an old man, introduces and sums up the story.

ACT 1. Three men from the homeward-bound merchantman *Rights o' Man* are impressed on board HMS *Indomitable*. They include Billy Budd (baritone), a seaman young, handsome, good, whose only flaw is a stammer. Claggart (bass), the master-at-arms, is detailed by Mr Redburn (baritone), the first lieutenant, to keep an eye on the new recruit, whose song of farewell to his old ship *Rights o' Man* is mistaken by the officers as a sign of incipient mutiny. Billy leads a chorus of praise for Captain Vere—Starry Vere, as he is known to his crew.

In his cabin, Vere is reading Plutarch. Mr Redburn and Mr Flint (baritone), the sailing master, arrive to take a glass of wine with him. They discuss the prospect of action against the French, and the recent naval mutinies sparked off by the French Revolution.

Meanwhile in the berth-deck the seamen are singing shanties, led by Billy, Red Whiskers (tenor) and Donald (baritone). Billy offers Dansker (bass), an old seaman who refuses to join in the singing, some tobacco from his kitbag, and there is a scuffle when he finds Squeak (tenor), a spy of Claggart's, apparently in the act of pilfering his possessions. The noise brings in the Master-at-Arms, who arrests Squeak, while the others sling their hammocks. Claggart sings of his intention to destroy Billy, whose goodness and beauty he cannot tolerate, and then instructs the Novice (tenor) to try and bribe Billy with French gold, inciting him to mutiny. The Novice, who has already been flogged once, dares not refuse. He wakens Billy and offers him the gold, but Billy's stammer rouses Dansker, and the Novice runs away.

ACT 2. Claggart seeks an interview with Captain Vere, to inform him that he has discovered a mutineer in the lower decks. Before he can name the seaman, an enemy ship is sighted, and Vere orders action stations.

A broadside is fired, but the enemy is still out of range. Then the mist comes down and the enemy escapes. The off-duty watch is dismissed, and Claggart continues his interview with the Captain. When Vere discovers that the mutineer is supposedly Billy Budd, he laughs at the idea, but agrees to interrogate Billy.

Billy and Claggart are brought before the Captain in his cabin. When the Master-at-Arms repeats his accusation, Billy is prevented from answering by his stammer and instead hits Claggart on the forehead, killing him. Vere, though convinced of Billy's innocence, summons a drumhead court, presided over by Mr Redburn. Vere is the only witness, but he refuses to influence the decision of the court. Billy is found guilty and sentenced to death by hanging from the yard-arm.

Billy, in irons in a bay of the gun-deck, sings a mournful farewell to the *Indomitable*. His mood is lightened by Dansker, who secretly brings his friend a mug of grog. The men are in a state of near-mutiny, he tells Billy. But Billy insists that he wants no trouble on his behalf; he had to strike down Claggart, and Captain Vere had to punish him—it was fate.

On deck the next morning, the ship's crew assembles. As Billy is marched on, there are sounds of discontent from the men, but Billy calls out 'Starry Vere, God bless you!' as he is led off to execution, and the crew takes up the cry. As Vere admits in the epilogue, he could have saved Billy, but in the event it was Billy who saved him.

Gloriana, opera in three acts with text by William Plomer, based on Lytton Strachey's *Elizabeth and Essex*. First produced on 8 June 1953 at Covent Garden. The opera covers the later years of the reign of Queen Elizabeth I.

The Turn of the Screw, opera in a prologue and two acts, with text by Myfanwy Piper after the story by Henry James. First performed on 14 September 1954 at

Teatro La Fenice, Venice. Set in the mid-nineteenth century.

PROLOGUE. The Governess (soprano) is engaged to look after two orphaned children by their uncle and guardian (tenor). She is to assume full responsibility and not worry him on any pretext.

ACT 1. The Governess arrives at Bly in Essex, and is greeted by Mrs Grose (mezzo-soprano), the housekeeper, Flora (soprano), aged eight, and Miles (treble), aged eleven. A letter arrives to say that Miles has been expelled from his school, but the Governess decides to say nothing. High up in one of the turrets of the house she sees a red-haired stranger. From the Governess's description, Mrs Grose identifies the man as Peter Quint, the Master's former valet, who had exercised an evil influence over Miles and had made Miss Jessel, Flora's previous governess, pregnant. But Quint, as well as Miss Jessel, is now dead. The Governess decides to resist Quint's evil power and then discovers, when teaching geography to Flora down by the lake, that the ghost of Miss Jessel also haunts Bly. Late at night Quint (tenor) summons Miles while Miss Jessel (mezzo-soprano) calls for Flora. The quartet becomes a sextet as the voices of Mrs Grose and the Governess are heard, seeking the children. The ghosts vanish.

ACT 2. Quint and Miss Jessel have an agitated colloquy. In the churchyard Miles and Flora sing a mock canticle, then Flora goes into church with Mrs Grose while Miles tells the Governess that he knows that she knows about the ghosts. Horrified, she rushes back to the house, meaning to leave Bly. But she finds Miss Jessel at her desk in the schoolroom, and changes her mind; she will write a letter, despite her instructions, to the children's guardian. In Miles's bedroom the governess tries to make the boy tell her what has happened, but Quint's menacing presence stops Miles from speaking. Quint orders the boy to steal and destroy the Governess's letter to the children's guardian. While Miles is playing the piano to an admiring audience of Mrs Grose and the Governess, Flora steals out of the house and down to the lake to meet Miss Jessel. Mrs Grose, who neither sees nor hears the ghosts, refuses at first to believe that the children are haunted, but by the next day she has changed her opinion and agrees to escort Flora to her guardian. The Governess remains with Miles, and struggles for his soul with Quint. Finally Miles accuses him, 'Peter Quint, you devil!' but dies in the Governess's arms.

Death in Venice, opera in two acts with text by Myfanwy Piper after Thomas Mann's story, *Tod in Venedig*. First performed on 16 June 1973 at Snape Maltings, Suffolk. The opera is set in Munich, Venice and the Lido during 1911. Gustav von Aschenbach (tenor), a famous German novelist, finds he has lost his ability to write.

ACT 1. Near a cemetery in Munich, Aschenbach meets a Traveller (baritone) who advises him to journey south.

On board ship, bound for Venice, Aschenbach is greeted by an Elderly Fop (baritone—the same singer as the Traveller) who joins a group of young men praising Venice, '*la Serenissima*'.

An old Gondolier (baritone—Traveller) rows Aschenbach to his hotel on the Lido.

At the hotel Aschenbach is greeted by the Manager (baritone—Traveller) and shown his room, with a magnificent view over the beach. The hotel guests assemble for dinner and Aschenbach notices a handsome Polish boy, Tadzio (dancer), with his mother, two sisters and their governess.

On the beach Aschenbach watches Tadzio, and again remarks on the boy's beauty and grace.

The sirocco is blowing and, finding Venice hot, dusty and full of beggars, importunate guides and noisy street-sellers, Aschenbach resolves to leave. He returns to his hotel to pack and then takes a gondola to the station, where he finds that his luggage has been put on the wrong train. He decides to go back to the Lido and wait there for the luggage.

On the beach Tadzio and his friends are playing. Aschenbach, in his deck-chair, imagines that he is watching the Greek Games of Apollo, and seems to hear the voice of Apollo (counter-tenor). Tadzio wins, and Aschenbach attempts to congratulate him, but cannot find words.

ACT 2. The hotel Barber (baritone—Traveller) hints to Aschenbach of a mysterious disease rife in Venice.

In the city Aschenbach picks up further rumours of sickness, including a German newspaper report that an outbreak of cholera has been officially denied. He sees the Polish family and follows them to a café, into St Mark's and back to the hotel. By now Aschenbach is infatuated with Tadzio.

After dinner, Strolling Players entertain the hotel guests. Aschenbach questions their Leader (baritone—Traveller) about the cholera, but is fobbed off with a song.

At the travel bureau, Aschenbach learns that cases of cholera have indeed occurred in Venice, and he is advised to leave.

Aschenbach feels that he should warn Tadzio's mother, the Lady of the Pearls (dancer), of the danger, but again fails to find words.

In a dream, Aschenbach hears the voices of Dionysus (baritone—Traveller) and Apollo, and participates in a Dionysian orgy.

Most of the guests have left, and Aschenbach watches Tadzio and a few friends playing on the near-deserted beach.

Aschenbach allows the hotel Barber to tint his grey hair and colour his cheeks with rouge.

In Venice, Aschenbach follows the Polish family again, and comes face to face with Tadzio. He buys some strawberries, but they are over-ripe.

At the hotel, Aschenbach learns from the Manager that the Polish family is leaving. He goes to the beach to watch Tadzio and his friends for the last time. The Polish boy is rolled in the sand by his companions and then runs off, as Aschenbach slumps dead in his deck-chair.

Busoni, Ferruccio (1866–1924), Italian composer. His operas were more appreciated in Germany and in other German-speaking countries than in Italy. *Die Brautwahl* (The Choice of a Bride), with text by the composer (who wrote all his own librettos) based on a story by E.T.A. Hoffmann, was first produced at Hamburg in 1912. *Arlecchino* (Harlequin), a one-act comedy with characters from the Commedia dell'arte, and *Turandot*, Busoni's two-act adaptation of the same fable by Gozzi that provided inspiration for Puccini's opera, were first performed in a double bill at Zurich in 1917. *Doktor Faust,* based not on Goethe's drama, but on Marlowe's play *Doctor Faustus* and on a German puppet-play of the eighteenth century, was left unfinished at the composer's death. Completed by Jarnach, it was first performed at Dresden in 1925.

Catalani, Alfredo (1854–93), Italian composer. While still a student in Milan, he composed a one-act opera *La falce* (The Sickle) with text by Boito, which was produced in the Conservatory theatre (1875). His first full-length opera, *Elda* (1880), was later revised and performed as *Loreley* (1890) at the Teatro Regio, Turin. *Dejanice* received three performances at La Scala, Milan

(1883), while the more successful *Edmea* (1886) was given eleven times at the same theatre. Catalani's most famous opera, *La Wally*, first performed at La Scala in 1892, is set in the Tyrol; hero and heroine, whose love is doomed to disappointment, perish in an avalanche.

Cavalli, Francesco (1602–76), Italian composer. He wrote more than 30 operas, most of them first performed in Venice. The most successful during Cavalli's lifetime were *Egisto* (1642), *Giasone* (1649), *Eritrea* (1653), *Ciro* (1654), *Xerse* (1655), *Erismena* (1656), *Artemesia* (1657) and *Scipione Affricana* (1664), all performed in several cities. Recently several of Cavalli's operas, unheard for three centuries, have been successfully revived, including *L'Ormindo* (1664) and *La Calisto* (1652), both of which scored popular hits at Glyndebourne.

Chabrier, Emmanuel (1841–94), French composer. He composed three comic operas: *L'Étoile* (The Star) (1877), *Une Education manquée* (An Incomplete Education) (1879), and *Le Roi malgré lui* (King In Spite of Himself), first produced in 1879 at the Opéra-Comique, Paris. Chabrier, an admirer of Wagner, also composed a grand opera, *Gwendoline*, to a libretto by Catulle Mendès, set in Saxon England. It was first performed in 1886 at the Théâtre de la Monnaie, Brussels. An unfinished opera, *Briseis*, was posthumously produced in 1899 at the Berlin State Opera, conducted by Richard Strauss.

Charpentier, Gustave, (1860–1956), French composer. His first opera, *Louise* (1900), was immensely successful, receiving more than a thousand performances at the Opéra-Comique during the composer's lifetime. Its sequel, *Julien* (1913), received only 20 during the same period.

Louise, opera in four acts with text by the composer. First produced on 2 February 1900 at the Opéra-Comique, Paris. Set in contemporary Paris.

ACT 1. In a poor quarter of Paris, Julien (tenor), an artist, tells Louise (soprano), the girl who lives opposite, how he came to fall in love with her. He has written to her Father asking for permission to marry her. Louise's Mother (mezzo-soprano) overhears some disparaging remarks about Julien, and calls Louise inside. Louise's Father (bass) returns exhausted from work, and the family sits down to supper. While Louise helps her mother to wash up, her father reads Julien's letter and says that she is still too young to think of getting married.

ACT 2. It is early morning. At the foot of the hill leading up to Montmartre, Rag-pickers, Street-sweepers and Street-sellers pursue their activities, while the Night-Prowler (tenor), a reveller in evening dress, symbolizes the pleasures of Paris. Julien and some friends come to wait for Louise, who works in a dressmaking establishment nearby. She arrives chaperoned by her Mother, and Julien hides until the Mother has left. He becomes very annoyed when Louise tells him that her parents will not consider his offer of marriage. Inside the workroom, the girls chatter as they sew, teasing Louise for being so obviously in love. Julien is heard serenading her from the street. Louise, suddenly making up her mind, puts on her coat and runs out to join him, to the amusement of the other girls.

ACT 3. Louise and Julien are living together in Montmartre. Louise expresses her happiness. The lights of Paris come on as the Bohemians arrive followed by the Night-Prowler dressed as the King of Fools. Louise is crowned Queen of Bohemia and Muse of Montmartre. The celebrations are cut short by the arrival of Louise's Mother, with news that her Father is very ill. Assured that she can return to Julien as soon as her Father is well again, Louise follows her Mother down the hill to Paris.

ACT 4. Louise's Father has just returned from the first day at work after his illness. He grumbles at the ingratitude of a daughter who does not appreciate the loving care of her parents. Louise, who has not been allowed to return to Julien, gazes out of the window at Paris and the freedom it offers. When she says goodnight to her Father, he sits her on his knee and embraces her as if she were still a child. She insists on her right to be free and in a fit of rage, he orders her out of the house. Louise runs off and her Father, regretting his action, calls her back. But she has escaped to Paris and freedom.

Cherubini, Luigi (1760–1842), Italian composer. After writing some dozen operas to Italian texts, produced in Italy and London, Cherubini went to Paris. His remaining operas, with one exception (*Faniska,* performed in Vienna, 1806), were settings of French texts, and were first produced in Paris. *Demóphoon* (1788) was given at the Opéra. *Lodoïska* (1791), *Medée* (1797) and *Les deux Journées* (1800), known in English as *The Water Carrier*, his three most successful operas, were premiered at the Théâtre Favart. *Medée* is an adaptation of Corneille's tragedy. Revenge is taken by Medea (soprano) on her former husband Jason (tenor), who has left her for Glauce (soprano), the daughter of King Creon (bass. This opera was originally composed with spoken dialogue separating the musical numbers. Sung recitatives were supplied by F. Lachner for a German performance in 1854, and by Arditi for an Italian performance in London in 1865, since when the opera has usually been given in that form.

Cilea, Francesco (1866–1950), Italian composer. Cilea's five operas were all well received on their first production, but only *L'arlesiana* (The Girl from Arles), an adaptation of Alphonse Daudet's play, first performed in 1897 at Milan (with Caruso), and *Adriana Lecouvreur* are now remembered.

Adriana Lecouvreur, opera in four acts with text by Arturo Colautti, from a play by Scribe and Legouvé. First performed on 6 November 1902 at Teatro Lirico, Milan. Set in Paris in 1730, the opera concerns the famous French actress Adrienne Lecouvreur.

ACT 1. Michonnet (baritone), stage director at the Comédie Française, is in love with Adriana (soprano), but she loves an unknown young cavalier who is in fact Maurizio, Count of Saxony (tenor). She gives him a bunch of violets and goes on stage for her performance. The Prince de Bouillon (bass), who is backstage to see his mistress, the actress Duclos, intercepts a letter making an assignation at Duclos' villa later that evening. The letter is from the Prince's wife, though he suspects his mistress.

ACT 2. In the villa, the Princess de Bouillon (mezzo-soprano) awaits Maurizio whom she loves. To pacify the Princess for his lateness he gives her the bunch of violets. Voices are heard and she hides in the adjoining room. Bouillon enters and is astonished to find Maurizio, apparently starting an affair with Duclos. Adriana now arrives, and is even more astounded to discover that Maurizio is the Count of Saxony. They start a passionate love scene, when Michonnet arrives, demanding to see Duclos on urgent theatrical business. Maurizio is forced to admit to Adriana that the lady in the next room is not Duclos. Adriana agrees to help her escape and, extinguishing the lights, tells her that the coast is clear. During their conversation in the dark, neither woman knowing the identity of the other, the Princess discovers that Adriana is also in love with Maurizio.

ACT 3. The Princess de Bouillon is giving a reception. When Adriana, one of the guests, arrives, the Princess recognizes her voice at once. She makes up a story of a duel in which Maurizio was gravely wounded, and Adriana is badly upset until Maurizio arrives in perfect health. The Princess makes it clear that she has first claim to Maurizio's attentions, but Adriana riposte with a recitation from Racine's *Phèdre* about an unfaithful wife.

ACT 4. Michonnet calls on Adriana to congratulate her on her birthday. The delivery of a casket containing the violets, now shrivelled and dead, that she had given Maurizio, upsets her. Maurizio himself comes in and swears not only that he loves her, but also that he wishes to marry her. After a brief moment of happiness, Adriana collapses—the violets, sent by the Princess, were poisoned—and dies in Maurizio's arms.

Cimarosa, Domenico (1749–1801), Italian composer. An enormously prolific composer, Cimarosa wrote over 60 operas. The only one that has stayed firmly in the repertory is *Il matrimonio segreto*, an adaptation by Bertati of the play *The Clandestine Marriage* by George Colman and David Garrick, in which the latter scored one of his greatest comic successes. First performed on 7 February 1792 at the Burgtheater, Vienna, *Il matrimonio segreto* concerns the troubles of Carolina (soprano) who is secretly married to Paolino (tenor), clerk to her father Don Geronimo (bass). A marriage has been arranged between Geronimo's other daughter, Elisetta (soprano), and the English Lord Robinson (baritone), who unfortunately prefers Carolina. Geronimo's elderly sister Fidalma (contralto), who nourishes a passion for Paolino, completes the cast.

Cornelius, Peter (1824–74), German composer. A friend and disciple of Liszt and Wagner, Cornelius composed two serious operas, *Der Cid* (1865), an adaptation of Corneille's tragedy *Le Cid*, and *Gunlöd*, with text taken from the *Edda*, posthumously produced at Weimar in 1891. But it is his comic opera, *Der Barbier von Bagdad*, with text by Cornelius taken from the Tale of the Tailor in *The Thousand and One Nights*, that has survived in the repertory, at least in Germany. A single, disastrous performance, conducted by Liszt, was given on its first production in Weimar on 15 December 1858. Abul Hassan Ali Ebn Bekar (baritone), the eponymous Barber, attempts to assist Nureddin (tenor) to gain an assignation with Margiana (soprano), daughter of the Cadi Baba Mustapha (tenor), but confuses the issue to such an extent that only the arrival of the Caliph (bass) can sort things out satisfactorily.

d'Albert, Eugen (1864–1932), German composer. Though born in Glasgow of French extraction, d'Albert was a composer in the German tradition. His 20 operas were all settings of German texts. The most successful, *Tiefland* (Lowland), first performed in 1903 at the German Theatre in Prague, is based on a Catalan play. Pedro (tenor), a shepherd in the High Pyrenees, descends to the valley to marry Marta (soprano), unaware that she is the mistress of Sebastiano (baritone), the local landowner. Marta confesses her past to Pedro and, when Sebastiano tries to resume relations with her, Pedro kills him and escapes with Marta back to the mountains.

Dallapiccola, Luigi (1904–75), Italian composer. He wrote three operas, *Volo di notte* (Night Flight), based on the novel by Antoine de Saint-Exupéry, first produced in 1940 in Florence; *Il prigioniero* (The Prisoner), first heard in 1949 on Italian radio and staged in 1950 in

Florence; and *Ulisse*, based on Homer's account of Odysseus' return home after the Trojan War, first performed in 1968 at the Deutsche Opèr, Berlin.

Debussy, Claude (1862–1918), French composer. His only opera, *Pelléas et Mélisande*, with text drawn by the composer from Maeterlinck's Symbolist play, was first performed on 30 April 1902 at the Opéra-Comique, Paris. The setting is the legendary kingdom of Allemonde, ruled over by the aged and nearly blind Arkel (bass). Golaud (baritone), the King's grandson, has married Mélisande (soprano), a young girl he found weeping by a pond in a wood. He is jealous of the sympathy between his wife and his half-brother Pelléas (high-baritone or tenor). With the aid of Yniold (soprano), his young son by a former marriage, Golaud spies on Melisande. Pelléas meets her by the fountain of the blind. They declare their mutual love but Golaud, who has followed them, kills Pelléas. Mélisande, delivered of a child, dies in the presence of Arkel and Golaud.

Delibes, Léo (1836–91), French composer. Perhaps best-known today for his ballet music, Delibes also wrote a number of popular operettas and six operas, including *Le Roi l'a dit* (The King Commanded It), first performed in 1873 at the Opéra-Comique, Paris, and the enormously successful *Lakmé*, which has received nearly 1,300 performances at the Opéra-Comique since its premiere on 14 April 1883. In three acts, with text by P. Gille and E. Gondinet, *Lakmé* is set in India in the nineteenth century. Gerald (tenor), an English officer, has fallen in love with Lakmé (soprano), daughter of Nilakantha (bass-baritone), a Brahmin priest, who is aware that a European has entered the holy temple precincts. In the bazaar, Lakmé is forced by her father to sing the famous Bell Song which, he hopes, will trap the European profaner into betraying his identity. Gerald duly appears and Lakmé faints. Nilakantha arranges to have the Englishman killed during a procession, but Gerald, only wounded, is nursed back to health by Lakmé in a hut in the forest. While she is fetching water from a holy spring, Gerald's fellow-officer Frederick (baritone) tells him that their regiment is leaving that night. Lakmé eats a leaf of the poisonous datura tree and, after swearing eternal love to Gerald, dies in his arms.

Delius, Frederick (1862–1934), English composer. The three most successful of Delius's six operas received their first performances in Germany: *Koanga* at Elberfeld in 1904; *A Village Romeo and Juliet* at the Komische Oper, Berlin, in 1907; and *Fennimore and Gerda* at Frankfurt in 1919. In England, thanks to the advocacy of Sir Thomas Beecham, *A Village Romeo and Juliet* has been the most frequently performed. The text is by the composer, based on a story by the Swiss writer Gottfried Keller. Sali (tenor) and Vreli (soprano), whose love is doomed because of the feud between their respective parents, Manz and Marti (baritones), over a patch of wild land dividing their properties, also claimed by the mysterious Dark Fiddler (baritone), dream of getting married and then spend a last day together before they drift down river in a barge, to drown, united in death.

Donizetti, Gaetano (1797–1848), Italian composer. Between 1818, when *Enrico di Borgogna*, his first opera (apart from student works), was staged in Venice, and 1830 Donizetti wrote some 30 operas, several of which were very successful at the time. The second, even more fruitful, half of his career was inaugurated with *Anna Bolena*, first performed on 26 December 1830 at Teatro

Carcano, Milan. Felice Romani's text was based on the quasi-historical disgrace and trial of Anne Boleyn (soprano), second wife of Henry VIII (bass), and on that monarch's growing love for Jane Seymour (soprano), later his third wife.

In the remaining 14 years of his active composing life, Donizetti produced another 35 operas, including several which have never been out of the repertory and some that have recently returned to popularity.

L'elisir d'amore (The Elixir of Love), comic opera in two acts, with text by Romani after Scribe's libretto *Le Philtre*. First performed on 12 May 1832 at Teatro della Canobbiana, Milan.

ACT 1. Nemorino (tenor), a young Italian peasant, is in love with Adina (soprano), a girl both rich and educated (he is neither) who reads aloud to the villagers the story of Tristan and Iseult. When Dulcamara (bass), a quack doctor, arrives in the village, Nemorino asks if he has a bottle of Iseult's elixir of love. Dulcamara sells Nemorino a flask of red wine, which gives him sufficient courage to stand up to Belcore (baritone), a dashing sergeant who is his rival with Adina.

ACT 2. Adina is celebrating her betrothal to Belcore, but seems strangely reluctant to sign the contract. Nemorino, in urgent need of another bottle of elixir but without the means to pay for it, enlists in the army to obtain some money. The second dose does the trick and the village girls pay court to him. (His rich uncle has died, though Nemorino is unaware of the fact.) Adina buys back his enlistment while Belcore and his men march out of the village, leaving Nemorino the victor.

Lucrezia Borgia, an adaptation by Romani of Victor Hugo's play about the celebrated Italian poisoner, was first performed on 26 December 1833 at La Scala, Milan. Alfonso d'Este (baritone) suspects his wife

Lucrezia (soprano) of being unfaithful to him with Gennaro (tenor), who is in fact her son. Forced by Alfonso to poison Gennaro, Lucrezia also gives him the antidote. At a banquet attended by Lucrezia's enemies, she poisons the wine unaware that Gennaro is among the company. This time he refuses the antidote, even when Lucrezia discloses their relationship, so she too drinks the wine and dies with him.

Maria Stuarda (1834) was another excursion into British history, with an unhistoric but dramatically effective confrontation between Mary Queen of Scots and Queen Elizabeth I at Fotheringay. Elizabeth I also appears in *Roberto Devereux* (1837), in which Robert, Earl of Essex (tenor), is secretly in love with Sarah, Duchess of Nottingham (mezzo-soprano), the wife of his friend the Duke (baritone). The Queen (soprano) discovers Robert's betrayal and he is sentenced to death. Elizabeth's subsequent intention of pardoning her favourite is thwarted by Nottingham, who ensures that Essex goes to the block.

Lucia di Lammermoor, opera in three acts with text by Salvatore Cammarano based on Walter Scott's novel *The Bride of Lammermoor*. First performed on 26 September 1835 at Teatro San Carlo, Naples. Set in Scotland about 1700.

ACT 1. Lucia, or Lucy Ashton, (soprano) is secretly in love with Edgar of Ravenswood (tenor), hereditary enemy of the Ashtons, who comes to say goodbye to her before an enforced absence in France.

ACT 2. Lucy's brother, Lord Henry Ashton (baritone), has arranged an advantageous marriage for her with Lord Arthur Bucklaw. To gain her consent, he tricks her with a forged letter into believing that Edgar has betrayed her. When Raymond (bass), or Bide-the-Bent, the chaplain, adds his persuasion, telling Lucy that it is her duty to obey her brother, she reluctantly agrees. Lord Arthur (tenor) arrives for the wedding, and the contract has just been signed, when Edgar appears. Shown Lucy's signature, he accuses her of betrayal.

ACT 3. Henry Ashton challenges Edgar to a fight the next day. Meanwhile Lucy, her mind unhinged, has killed Lord Arthur in their apartment and descends to the hall where the wedding guests are still feasting, to sing the most famous mad-scene in all opera.

In the churchyard where his ancestors are buried, Edgar waits in vain for Henry. Raymond arrives instead, with the news that Lucy is dead. With nothing left to live for, Edgar kills himself with his dagger.

La Fille du régiment (The Daughter of the Regiment), opera in two acts with text (in French) by Vernoy de St George and F. Bayard. First performed on 11 February 1840 at the Opéra-Comique, Paris. Set in the Swiss Tyrol about 1815.

ACT 1. Marie (soprano) has been adopted by a regiment of French Grenadiers. Tonio (tenor), a young peasant in love with Marie, joins the Grenadiers in order to remain near her. The Marquise de Birkenfeld (mezzo-soprano) demands a safe-conduct through the French lines. Sergeant Sulpice (bass), recognizing her name, gives her some papers that were found with the infant Marie. The Marquise declares that Marie is her niece and takes her to live at Birkenfeld.

ACT 2. At the castle, Marie is being taught dancing and other ladylike accomplishments. With Sulpice, who has accompanied her to Birkenfeld, she breaks out into the Song of the Regiment. The Grenadiers, led by Tonio, now promoted to captain, arrive to visit Marie. The Marquise wishes Marie to marry a nobleman and, when she confesses that Marie is really her daughter, the girl feels obliged to obey her mother. But at the betrothal party Marie fondly reminisces about her childhood with the Grenadiers; the Marquise, realizing where her daughter's heart really lies, gives her to Tonio instead.

Donizetti's other operas to French texts are *La Favorite* and *Les Martyrs*, both performed in 1840 at the Paris Opéra. *La Favorite* takes place in fourteenth-century Spain at the court of Alfonso XI of Castile (baritone), whose mistress Leonora de Gusman (mezzo-soprano) is in love with Ferdinand (tenor), a novice at the monastery of St James. *Les Martyrs* is a four-act grand opera with text by Scribe based on Corneille's tragedy *Polyeucte*. *Poliuto*, the Italian version of *Les Martyrs*, composed in 1839, was not performed until 1848, at Naples.

Don Pasquale, comic opera in three acts, with text by G. Ruffini and the composer. First performed on 3 January 1843 at the Théâtre-Italien, Paris. Set in Rome.

ACT 1. Don Pasquale (bass), an elderly bachelor, plans to get married, to the chagrin of his nephew and heir, Ernesto (tenor), who wishes to marry Norina (soprano), a young widow. Dr Malatesta (baritone) announces that he has found Pasquale a bride—his own sister, straight out of a convent. Malatesta plans to introduce Norina as Sophronia, his imaginary sister, and, learning that Pasquale has disinherited Ernesto, she enters enthusiastically into the plan.

ACT 2. Pasquale is enchanted with his beautiful but timid bride. Ernesto is brought in as a witness and recognizes Norina. He is in despair until, the moment the contract is signed (before a false notary), she erupts in a furious temper finding fault with everything. Pasquale is aghast at the termagant he has married.

ACT 3. The new mistress of the household, having ordered clothes, jewels, a carriage and horses, goes off to the opera, carefully dropping a note for an assignation in the garden that evening. Pasquale sends for Malatesta, who pretends to be shocked and horrified. In the garden, Ernesto keeps the assignation with Norina. Pasquale is so relieved to discover that he is not really married to 'Sophronia' that he reinstates Ernesto as heir and blesses his marriage to Norina.

Dukas, Paul (1865–1935), French composer. His only opera, *Ariane et Barbe-Bleue* (Ariadne and Bluebeard); an adaptation of Maeterlinck's play of the same name, was first performed on 10 May 1907 at the Opéra-Comique, Paris, and was taken into the repertory of the Opéra in 1935.

Dvořák, Antonin (1841–1904), Czech composer. His ten operas include *The Peasant and the Rogue* (1878); *Dimitrij* (1882), an historical drama about the pretender to the Russian throne who rebelled against Boris Godunov; *The Jacobin* (1889), a comedy in which the exiled protagonist, who is not in fact a Jacobin, returns home and is reconciled with his father; and *The Devil and Kate* (1899). These operas were all first performed in Prague at the Czech, later the National, Theatre, as was Dvořák's operatic masterpiece *Rusalka* (1901), based on De la Motte Fouquet's *Undine*, the legend of a water sprite who falls in love with a mortal.

Einem, Gottfried von (born 1918), Austrian composer. His very successful operas include *Dantons Tod*, an adaptation by Boris Blacher of Georg Büchner's play *The Death of Danton*, first performed in 1947 at Salzburg; *Der Prozeß*, based on Kafka's novel *The Trial*, first performed in 1953, also at Salzburg; *Der Besuch der alten Dame*, an adaptation of F. Dürrenmatt's play *The Visit of the Old Lady*, first produced in 1971 at the Vienna State Opera; and *Kabale und Liebe*, adapted from Schiller's drama *Intrigue and Love*, staged in 1976, again in Vienna.

Falla, Manuel de (1876–1946), Spanish composer. His first opera, *La Vida breve* (Brief Life), first performed (in French) at Nice in 1913, remains his most successful. *El Retablo de Maese Pedro* (Master Peter's Puppet-Show), a one-act opera with text by the composer, derived from Cervantes' novel *Don Quixote*, was first heard in concert at Seville in 1923, and staged privately in Paris (in French) later the same year. *L'Atlantida*, unfinished at the composer's death, was completed by Halffter, heard in concert at Barcelona in 1961 and staged at La Scala, Milan, the following year.

Fauré, Gabriel (1845–1924), French composer. Apart from *Prométhée*, a 'Greek tragedy', partly spoken and partly sung, first performed in 1900 in the Béziers Arena and later (1907) given at the Paris Opéra, Fauré wrote only one opera, *Pénélope*, first performed on 4 March 1913 at Monte Carlo. The theme, taken from Homer, of Odysseus' homecoming after the Trojan War, is one that has attracted composers from Monteverdi to Dallapiccola.

Flotow, Friedrich von (1812–83), German composer. His early operas were mainly settings of French texts and were first performed in Paris. His two best-known operas, though based on works from the earlier French period, have German texts. *Alessandro Stradella*, first performed in 1844 at Hamburg, deals with the highly coloured life of the seventeenth-century Italian composer. *Martha*, based on the ballet *Lady Henriette ou la Servante de Greenwich*, for which Flotow composed some music, was first produced on 25 November 1847 at the Kärntnertortheater, Vienna. Subtitled 'Richmond Fair', *Martha* describes the adventures of Lady Harriet (soprano), maid of honour to Queen Anne, and her own maid Nancy (mezzo-soprano), who disguise themselves as servants, Martha and Julia, and are hired by two young farmers, Lionel (tenor) and Plunkett (bass).

Gershwin, George (1898–1937), American composer. Apart from the jazz one-acter *Blue Monday*, later renamed *125th Street*, Gershwin's only opera was *Porgy and Bess*, the first composed for an all-black cast. With text in three acts by DuBose Heyward and Ira Gershwin, it was first performed on 30 September 1935 at the Colonial Theatre, Boston. The scene is Catfish Row, Charleston, South Carolina. Porgy (bass-baritone), a cripple, is in love with Bess (soprano), who is Crown's girl. Crown (bass), a stevedore, kills Robbins (tenor) during a game of dice, and leaves to escape the police. Bess takes shelter with Porgy. Peter (tenor), the old Honeyman, is arrested as a material witness to Robbins's murder. Sportin' Life (tenor), a gambler, tries to bribe Bess with dope to go with him to New York, but Porgy threatens to kill him if he doesn't leave Bess alone.

The inhabitants of Catfish Row all go on a picnic, except for Porgy. On Kittiwah Island, Bess is approached by Crown, who has been hiding there, and stays behind with him when the boat takes the other picnickers home.

Peter is let out of jail, and Bess, after two days, returns to Porgy. During a great storm Jake (baritone), a fisherman, and Clara (contralto), his wife, are lost. Crown returns for Bess, but is killed by Porgy.

The police take Porgy away to identify the body, and he is jailed for a week for contempt of court for refusing to look at Crown. On his return to Catfish Row he finds that Bess has gone off with Sportin' Life, seduced by the 'happy dust'.

Giordano, Umberto (1867–1948), Italian composer. The first of his operas to be performed, *Mala vita*

(Underworld), given at Rome in 1892, established Giordano's style in the veristic tradition; his third opera, *Andrea Chénier* (1896) brought the composer worldwide fame. Though *Fedora* (1898) and *Siberia*, produced in 1905 at La Scala, Milan, were initially popular, none of Giordano's later operas achieved the success of *Andrea Chénier*. *Madame Sans-Gêne*, premiered at the Metropolitan, New York, in 1915, was conducted by Arturo Toscanini, who also introduced Giordano's last opera, *Il re* (The King), at La Scala in 1929.

Andrea Chénier, opera in four acts with text by Luigi Illica. First performed on 28 March 1896 at La Scala, Milan. Set in Paris before and during the Revolution.

ACT 1. The poet André Chénier (tenor) attends a reception given by the Countess de Coigny (mezzo-soprano); at the request of her daughter Madeleine (soprano) he improvises a poem. Gérard (baritone), one of the servants, leads in some beggars, who are evicted without disturbing the guests.

ACT 2. The Revolution has begun and Chénier's life is in danger. Refusing to leave Paris, he keeps an assignation at the Cafe Hottot with an unknown correspondent; it is Madeleine, and she and Chénier sing of their mutual love. Gérard, now a leading revolutionary, also loves Madeleine; in a fight with Chénier he is wounded.

ACT 3. At the hearing of the Revolutionary Tribunal, Gérard makes an impassioned speech. He debates whether to denounce Chénier, then in a fit of jealousy signs the indictment. Madeleine comes to beg for Chénier's life, offering herself to Gérard in exchange for the poet's freedom. She describes her mother's death at the hands of the mob. Chénier, brought before the Tribunal, is sentenced to death despite Gérard's pleading on his behalf.

ACT 4. In the prison of St Lazare, Chénier writes a

poem welcoming death. Gérard brings in Madeleine, bribing the jailer to let her replace one of the female prisoners. Chénier and Madeleine go to the guillotine together.

Glinka, Mikhail Ivanovich (1804–57), Russian composer. The father of Russian music, as he has been called, wrote two works from which descend the mainstreams of Russian national opera: the historical and the legendary.

A Life for the Tsar, or *Ivan Susanin*, opera in four acts with text by G. F. Rosen. First performed on 9 December 1836 in St Petersburg. Set in Russia and Poland during the winter of 1612.

ACT 1. Antonida (soprano), daughter of Ivan Susanin (bass), celebrates the return of her betrothed, Sobinjin (tenor), from the wars. News comes that a Polish army is advancing on Moscow, though it has been temporarily checked. Antonida and Sobinjin plan to get married at once.

ACT 2. In the Polish camp a magnificent ball is taking place. Word is brought that Romanov has been elected Tsar, and the Poles plan to capture him.

ACT 3. In Susanin's house, the wedding celebrations are interrupted by the arrival of Polish troops. They want Susanin to show them the way to the monastery where the Tsar is living. He pretends to agree, secretly telling Vanja (contralto), his adopted son, to warn the Tsar, while he leads the Poles astray.

ACT 4. In the snow-covered forest Susanin has successfully misled the Polish troops. When they discover this, they kill him.

Antonida, Sobinjin and Vanja join the crowds in Moscow waiting to welcome the Tsar, whose procession is approaching the Kremlin.

Russlan and Ludmila, opera in five acts with text by

Shirkov and Bakhturin based on a poem by Pushkin. First performed on 9 December 1842 in St Petersburg.

Three suitors wish to marry Ludmila (soprano), daughter of the Prince of Kiev (bass). When Ludmila disappears, the Prince offers her hand to the suitor who can rescue her. Russlan (tenor), a knight, seeks the aid of Finn (tenor), a good fairy. After many adventures, he rescues Ludmila from the castle of the wicked dwarf Chernemor (silent role).

Gluck, Christoph Willibald von (1714–87), German composer. He wrote some 30 operas, serious or comic, to Italian or French texts, that were produced in Italy, London, or Vienna, before embarking on his first so-called reform opera *Orfeo ed Euridice* (1762) in which he attempted to combine the music and drama more closely. Several conventional pieces followed, then after *Alceste* (1767) and *Paride e Elena* (Paris and Helen), his last opera for Vienna, in 1770, Gluck abandoned Italian opera altogether. The rest of his works, settings of French texts, were all composed for Paris. They include *Iphigénie en Aulide* (1773), the French versions of *Orphée et Euridice* and *Alceste*, *Armide* (1777) and *Iphigénie en Tauride* (1779).

Orfeo ed Euridice (Orpheus and Eurydice), opera in three acts with text by Ranieri de' Calzabigi. First performed on 5 October 1762 at the Burgtheater, Vienna; French version on 2 August 1774 at the Paris Opéra. Based on the Greek legend.

ACT 1. Orpheus (contralto; in French version, tenor) laments the loss of his bride Eurydice. Amor (soprano), the God of Love, tells him that he may descend to the Underworld to fetch Eurydice, but he must not look at her until they are back across the River Styx.

ACT 2. At the entrance to Hades, Orpheus sings so sweetly to the Furies that they let him through into the

Elysian Fields, where the Happy Shades bring Eurydice (soprano) to him. Without looking at her, Orpheus takes his bride by the hand and leads her away.

ACT 3. Eurydice cannot understand why Orpheus will not look at her and protests so piteously that, forgetting the warning of Amor, Orpheus turns to her. At once she dies. Orpheus again laments the death of his bride and once more Amor takes compassion on him, restoring Eurydice to life.

Alceste (Alcestis), opera in three acts with text by Calzabigi after the tragedy by Euripedes. First performed on 26 December 1767 at the Burgtheater, Vienna; French version, with the text by L. du Roullet, on 23 April 1776 at the Paris Opéra.

ACT 1. Despite the prayers of his wife, Alcestis (soprano), and of his people, King Admetus (tenor) is near to death. The High Priest (baritone) invokes the Oracle in the Temple of Apollo, which announces that Admetus can be saved if a friend dies in his place. Alcestis offers her own life for her husband's.

ACT 2. The King's recovery is being celebrated. Evander (tenor) tells Admetus of the terms imposed by the Oracle, but does not name the victim. Alcestis cannot hide her grief at the thought of leaving her husband and children. Finally she confesses that she is the victim. Admetus refuses to accept her sacrifice. He will follow her down to Hades.

ACT 3. The people mourn their King and Queen. Hercules (baritone), who has just completed his Labours, is aghast to hear that Admetus is dead. At the Gates of Hell, Alcestis pleads to be admitted. Admetus arrives in pursuit, but she is determined to save him. Hercules now comes to help rescue Alcestis. Apollo, announcing that Hercules has won a place among the Gods, restores both Alcestis and Admetus to Earth. He bids the people rejoice.

Gounod, Charles (1818–93), French composer. The first two of his 12 operas, *Sapho* (1851) and *La Nonne sanglante* (1854), based on *The Monk*, the gothic novel by M. G. Lewis, were relative failures at the Paris Opéra. *Le Medecin malgré lui* (The Mock Doctor) fared better in 1858 at the Théâtre-Lyrique, where the following year *Faust*, for over half a century the most popular opera in the world, began its triumphant career. Gounod's next three operas scored little success, but *Mireille* (1864), which some consider his finest work in its perfect matching of music to subject, and *Roméo et Juliette* (1867) were very well received.

Faust, Opera in five acts with text by Jules Barbier and Michel Carré, based on Goethe's poetic drama. First performed on 19 March 1859 at the Théâtre-Lyrique, Paris. Set in sixteenth-century Germany.

ACT 1. In his study, Faust (tenor) laments his lost youth and calls on the Devil to help him regain it. Mephistopheles (bass) appears and offers Faust eternal youth and the love of Marguerite, seen in a vision, in exchange for Faust's soul. The bargain is signed.

ACT 2. Outside the town, citizens and soldiers celebrate the Fair. Mephistopheles angers Valentine (baritone) by drinking the health of his sister Marguerite. Valentine's sword is broken in the ensuing duel but, by holding the hilt as a cross, he renders Mephistopheles helpless. Faust meets Marguerite returning from church, but she refuses his escort. The crowd dances.

ACT 3. Siebel (mezzo-soprano), a youth in love with Marguerite, lays flowers on her doorstep. Mephistopheles, on behalf of Faust, replaces them with a grander bouquet and a casket of jewels. Marguerite, sitting at her spinning wheel, sings the ballad of the King of Thule. She sees the casket, opens it, and tries on the jewels. While Martha (mezzo-soprano), Marguerite's neighbour, is entertained by Mephistopheles, Faust expresses his love to Marguerite. She goes into the house, but at the open window confesses her love for the handsome stranger. Faust rushes to embrace her.

ACT 4. Marguerite has been betrayed and abandoned by Faust but still loves him. In the cathedral, her prayers are interrupted by the mocking voice of Mephistopheles. The soldiers return from the war and Valentine learns of his sister's dishonour. Mortally wounded in a duel with Faust, he curses Marguerite.

ACT 5. Marguerite is in prison, condemned to death for killing her child. Faust and Mephistopheles come to free her, but she refuses to accompany them and, calling on the angels, dies, to be carried up to Heaven.

Mireille, opera in five acts with text by Michel Carré based on the poem *Mireio* by Frédéric Mistral. First performed on 19 March 1864 at the Théâtre-Lyrique, Paris. Set in Arles and other districts of Provence.

Mireille (soprano), daughter of Maître Ramon (bass), is in love with Vincent (tenor), though her father wishes her to marry Ourrias (baritone), a bull-tender. Despite a warning from the old woman Taven (mezzo-soprano), Mireille and Vincent pledge their love for each other.

Vincent and Ourrias fight in the Val d'enfer; Vincent is wounded but sheltered by Taven in her cave nearby, and Ourrias drowns in the Rhône. Mireille, escaping from her father, makes her way across the desert of Crau to the church of the Saintes-Maries, where she is to meet Vincent. Exhausted by the heat, she dies in her lover's arms.

Roméo et Juliette, opera in five acts with text by Barbier and Carré based on Shakespeare's tragedy, which it follows closely. First performed on 27 April 1867 at the Théâtre-Lyrique.

Grétry, André (1741–1813), Belgian composer. He wrote over 50 operas, nearly all first produced in Paris,

Versailles or Fontainebleau. Among the most successful were *Zémire et Azore* (1771), a version of Beauty and the Beast, *L'Amant jaloux* (1778) and *Richard Coeur-de-Lion* (1784), Grétry's masterpiece. This recounts a fictitious event in the life of Richard I of England and includes the episode of the King's rescue by his minstrel Blondel.

Halévy, Fromental (1799–1862), French composer. His 30 operas include several that were enormously successful in their day, though Halévy is now remembered only for *La Juive* (The Jewess). This grand opera in five acts, with text by Eugène Scribe, was first produced on 23 February 1835 at the Paris Opéra, where it achieved 500 performances well before the end of the century. Set in fifteenth-century Constance, the opera has as protagonist Rachel (soprano), supposed enormously to Eléazar (tenor), a Jewish goldsmith. Rachel is sentenced to death by Cardinal Brogni (bass) for consorting with a Christian, Leopold (tenor), who works in Eléazar's workshop disguised as a Jew, Samuel. Leopold loves Rachel, though he is married to Eudoxie (soprano), the Emperor's niece. Rachel is thrown into a boiling cauldron as Eléazar reveals that she is not his daughter but the Cardinal's.

Handel, George Frideric (1685–1759), German, later naturalized English, composer. His first operas, *Almira* and *Nero* (1705), were produced in Hamburg, where Handel played in the orchestra as second violinist and, later, harpsichordist. After travelling to Italy, where *Rodrigo* (1707) was performed at Florence, and *Agrippina* (1709) at Venice, Handel paid his first visit to England, where he was to live for most of the rest of his life, composing some 36 Italian operas over the next 30 years. These include *Rinaldo* (1711), *Radamisto* (1720), *Giulio Cesare* (1724), *Rodelinda* (1725), *Alessandro* (1726),

Ezio (1732), *Orlando* (1733), *Ariodante* (1735), *Alcina* (1735), *Serse* (1738) and *Deidamia* (1741). Of these, the operas most frequently revived today are *Giulio Cesare*, in which Cleopatra (soprano), Queen of Egypt, is saved from the clutches of her brother Ptolemy (contralto) by Julius Caesar (contralto), who has fallen in love with her; and *Alcina*, derived from Ariosto's *Orlando furioso*, in which Bradamante (contralto), disguised as her brother Ricciardo, endeavours to save her betrothed, Ruggiero (soprano), from the power of the beautiful sorceress Alcina (soprano). Handel's oratorios, settings of English texts, have also been staged. These include *Saul* (1739), *Samson* (1743), *Semele* (1744), *Hercules* (1745) and *Jephtha* (1744).

Haydn, Joseph (1732–1809), Austrian composer. Written for performance in the private theatre at Esterházy, where Haydn was employed by Prince Nicholas Esterházy, his operas are mainly comedies, settings of Italian texts, and have for long been considered undramatic. Modern revivals have shown that most of them are still stageworthy, including *Lo speziale* (The Apothecary) (1768), *Le pescatrici* (The Fisherwomen) (1769), *L'infedeltà delusa* (The Deceptive Infidelity) (1773), *Il mondo della luna* (The World of the Moon) (1777) and *La fedeltà premiata* (Fidelity Rewarded) (1780).

Henze, Hans Werner (born 1926), German composer. He has written seven full-length operas, as well as a number of shorter music-theatre pieces.
Boulevard Solitude, in seven scenes, with text (in German) by Grete Weil. First performed on 17 February 1952 at Hanover. It is a modern version of Prévost's *Manon Lescaut*, set in Paris in the immediate post-World War II period.

König Hirsch (King Stag), in three acts with text by Heinz von Cremer. First performed on 23 September 1956 at the Städtische Oper, Berlin. Based on the fable *Il re cervo* by Carlo Gozzi.

Der Prinz von Homburg, in three acts with text by Ingeborg Bachmann. First produced on 22 May 1960 at Hamburg Staatsoper. It is an adaptation of *Prince Frederick of Homburg*, a play by Heinrich von Kleist, in which the protagonist is court-martialled and sentenced to death for dereliction of duty on the battlefield, but is eventually pardoned.

Elegy for Young Lovers, in five acts with text (in English) by W. H. Auden and Chester Kallman. First performed (in German translation) on 20 May 1961 at Schwetzingen; first English performance on 19 July 1961 at Glyndebourne. Set in the Austrian Alps in 1910. Gregor Mittenhofer (baritone), a poet and a monstrous example of the romantic concept of the Artist as Hero, takes the deaths of Elisabeth Zimmermann (soprano), his mistress, and Toni Reischmann (tenor), with whom she is in love, as inspiration for his new poem, Elegy for Young Lovers.

Der junge Lord, in two acts with text by Ingeborg Bachmann. First performed on 7 April 1965 at Deutsche Oper, Berlin. Set in a small German town about 1830. Sir Edgar (silent role), a rich Englishman, arrives in Hülsdorf-Gotha with his nephew Lord Barrat (tenor), his Secretary (baritone) and his Jamaican cook Begonia (mezzo-soprano). Local society, headed by Baroness Grünwiesel (mezzo-soprano), is invited by Sir Edgar to a reception to meet his nephew. Despite Lord Barrat's uncouth manners, Luise (soprano), the Baroness's ward, is impressed by him, to the chagrin of her admirer Wilhelm (tenor), a student. In the ballroom of Sir Edgar's house a dance is in progress. Lord Barrat dances with Luise, to whom he has become engaged, so energetically that she falls exhausted. Lord Barrat tears off his smart clothes, revealing that he is an ape.

The Bassarids, in one act with intermezzo; text (in English) by Auden and Kallman, based on *The Bacchae* of Euripides. First performed (in German translation) on 6 August 1966 at Salzburg; first English performance on 7 August 1968 at Santa Fe.

Pentheus (baritone), in his first proclamation as King of Thebes, announces that as neither Semele, the dead sister of his mother Agave (mezzo-soprano), nor her lover (in fact Zeus) was an immortal, their offspring Dionysus is not a god. He orders his guards to take prisoner anyone found worshipping Dionysus on Mount Cythaeron. The prisoners include Agave, her sister Autonoe (soprano), the blind prophet Tiresias (tenor) and a young stranger (tenor), who is Dionysus himself. An earthquake opens the door to the prison and all the prisoners escape.

As intermezzo, several of the characters re-enact the Judgement of Calliope.

Pentheus, determined to discover what goes on during the Bacchic rites on Mount Cythaeron, dresses as a woman and hides in a tree to watch the orgy. The Maenads, led by Agave, are warned by Dionysus that a stranger is in their midst. Pentheus is pursued, caught, and torn limb from limb. Agave arrives back in Thebes carrying her son's head. Dionysus, his mother Semele avenged, orders Thebes to be burnt to the ground.

We Come to the River, in two parts, with text (in English) by Edward Bond. First performed on 12 July 1976 at Covent Garden. Set in Europe during the nineteenth century and later.

PART 1. A General (bass-baritone), who has just won a victory, is told by a Doctor (bass) that he is going blind. A Deserter (tenor) is shot. The General visits the battlefield, where a Young Woman (soprano) with a child is searching for her husband. The Governor (bass) is taking a parade and offers congratulations to the General, who behaves strangely. The General returns to the battlefield to talk to the Young Woman, who is shot as a looter. The General is taken away by the Doctor and the Governor. Soldiers chase the Old Woman (mezzo-soprano) who is carrying the Young Woman's child, into the river, and shoot her.

PART 2. The General is in a madhouse, surrounded by mad people. The Second Soldier (tenor) from the firing squad, now a civilian, comes to visit the General. There is civil war in the provinces and the Governor also visits the General to enlist his help, which the General refuses. The Governor reports back to his ministers; as he leaves the meeting, he is shot by the Second Soldier. The Emperor (contralto) is having a picnic by the river with girls in white. He resolves to blind the General. Two assassins carry out the task in the madhouse. The General, at last, can see. He is joined by the Deserter and the Young Woman, who is the Deserter's wife, the Old Woman and the child. The mad people accuse the General of being a spy. They metaphorically drown him in the river by burying him in white sheets.

Hérold, Ferdinand (1791–1833), French composer. He contributed 20 operas, alone or in collaboration, to the repertories of the Opéra-Comique and the Opéra. His reputation rests on *Zampa*, first performed on 2 May 1831 at the Opéra-Comique, and *Le Pré au clercs*, first produced on 15 December 1832 at the same theatre, where the 1,580th performance took place exactly a century after its premiere.

Hindemith, Paul (1895–1963), German, later naturalized American, composer. His first three operas,

Cardillac (1926), *Hin und Zurück* (There and Back) (1927) and *Neues vom Tage* (1929), were produced in Germany but his best-known work, *Mathis der Maler*, composed in 1934, was banned in Nazi Germany and first performed at Zurich in 1938. *Die Harmonie der Welt*, a study of the astronomer Kepler, was produced in 1957 at Munich; and *The Long Christmas Dinner*, based on Thornton Wilder's play, was produced in 1961 at Mannheim.

Cardillac, an opera in three acts with text by F. Lion, based on E.T.A. Hoffmann's story *Das Fräulein von Scuderi*. First performed on 9 November 1926 at Dresden; revised version on 20 June 1952 at Zurich. Cardillac (baritone), a goldsmith, cannot bear to part with the jewellery that he makes and murders each customer after a sale.

Neues vom Tage (News of the Day), comic opera in three parts with text by M. Schiffer. First performed on 8 June 1929 at the Kroll Oper, Berlin. The matrimonial difficulties of Laura (soprano) and Eduard (baritone) are exploited by Baron d'Houdoux (bass), head of a publicity firm. Despite the efficient services of Hermann (tenor), a professional co-respondent, the couple manage to stay married.

Mathis der Maler (Mathis the Painter), opera in seven scenes with text by the composer. First performed on 28 May 1938 in Zurich. Set in Germany in the sixteenth century. Matthias Grünewald (baritone), the Master of the Isenheim Altarpiece, who is in the service of Cardinal Albrecht (tenor), Archbishop of Mainz, gets involved in the Peasants' Rebellion by helping Schwalb (tenor), the peasants' leader, and his daughter Regina (soprano). When Schwalb is killed, Mathis escapes with Regina and, after a vision of the Temptation of St Anthony, in which the Cardinal appears as St Paul, he resolves to reject politics and return to art, his true vocation.

Mascagni Cavalleria rusticana. Royal Opera Covent Garden, 1976. Santuzza (Pauline Tinsley), Turiddu (Placido Domingo) (Donald Southern)

(*right*) Monteverdi *Orfeo* (La favola d'Orfeo). English National Opera, 1981. Eurydice (Patricia O'Neill), Orfeo (Anthony Rolfe Johnson) (Reg Wilson)

(*below*) Mozart *Le nozze di Figaro*. Glyndebourne, 1981. Cherubino (Faith Esham), Countess (Isobel Buchanan) (Guy Gravett)

(*right*) Mozart *Così fan tutte*. Glyndebourne, 1979. Guglielmo (Alan Titus), Fiordiligi (Bozena Betley), Don Alfonso (Stafford Dean), Dorabella (Patricia Parker), Ferrando (John Aler) (Guy Gravett)

(*right*) Mozart *Don Giovanni*. Glyndebourne, 1977. Don Giovanni (Benjamin Luxon)

(*above*) Puccini *La Bohème*. Royal Opera Covent Garden, 1980. Alcindoro (Eric Garrett), Musetta (Carol Neblett), Marcello (Peter Glossop), Rodolfo (Peter Dvorsky), Mimi (MIrella Freni), Schaunard (John Rawnsley), Colline (Gwynne Howell) (Donald Southern)

(*below*) Mozart *La clemenza di Tito*. Royal Opera Covent Garden, 1976. Vitellia (Janet Baker), Sesto (Yvonne Minton) (Donald Southern)

Holst, Gustav (1874–1934), English composer. His first five operas remain unpublished and mainly unperformed, but the following, all in one act, have been successfully revived: *Savitri* (1916) is a chamber opera with text by the composer based on an episode in the Indian epic *Mahabharata*. *The Perfect Fool* (1923) is a comic piece that parodies operatic conventions. *At the Boar's Head* (1925) has a text drawn from the Falstaff episodes in Shakespeare's *Henry IV*, parts 1 and 2. *The Wandering Scholar* (1934) is adapted from a chapter in Helen Waddell's *The Wandering Scholars*.

Humperdinck, Engelbert (1854–1921), German composer. The first of his seven operas, *Hänsel und Gretel* (1893), was much the most successful and has retained its popularity. *Königskinder* (Royal Children), was first produced on 28 December 1910 at the Metropolitan, New York. A Goose-Girl (soprano), who has been brought up by a Witch (contralto), but is in reality a princess, falls in love with a King's Son (tenor), who is disguised as a beggar. Eventually the two royal children die together in a snowstorm.

Hänsel und Gretel, opera in three acts with text by Adelheid Wette based on a tale by the Brothers Grimm. First performed on 23 December 1893 at the Hoftheater, Weimar, conducted by Richard Strauss.

Hänsel (mezzo-soprano) and Gretel (soprano), the children of Peter (baritone), a poor broom-maker, and his wife Gertrude (soprano), are lost in the wood where they have been sent to gather strawberries. They lie down to sleep, guarded by angels, and in the morning wake to find a gingerbread house, inhabited by a Witch (mezzo-soprano). The Witch puts Hänsel in a cage to fatten him up for baking. The children manage to push the Witch into her own oven, and the gingerbread figures of the other missing children come to life just as Peter and Gertrude arrive on the scene.

Ibert, Jacques (1890–1962), French composer. His operas include *Angélique*, a one-act farce first performed on 28 January 1927 at the Théâtre-Femina, Paris, and *L'Aiglon* (The Eaglet), composed in collaboration with Arthur Honegger. Ibert wrote Acts 1 and 5, Honegger Acts 2, 3 and 4. The text, by Henri Cain, is based on Edmond Rostand's play about the Duke of Reichstadt, Napoleon's son. The opera was first performed on 11 March 1937 at Monte Carlo.

Janáček, Leoš (1854–1928), Czech composer. His third opera, *Jenufa* (composed between 1884 and 1903), was the first to be produced. Its successful revival in 1916 at Prague encouraged Janáček to complete *Mr Brouček's Excursion to the Moon*, on which he had been at work for eight years. He also wrote the second part, *Mr Brouček's Excursion to the XVth Century* (1918), and composed four more operas, *Katya Kabanova*, *The Cunning Little Vixen*, *The Makropulos Case* and *From the House of the Dead*, during the last decade of his life.

Jenufa, or *Her Foster-Daughter*, opera in three acts with text by the composer after a play by Gabriela Preissová. First performed on 21 January 1904 at Brno. Set in the Moravian mountains.

ACT 1. At the mill owned by Grandmother Buryja (contralto), Jenufa (soprano), who is secretly expecting a child by her cousin Števa (tenor), waits anxiously to hear if Števa has been taken for military service. She is watched by Laca (tenor), Števa's stepbrother, who loves Jenufa, though he will not admit it, even to himself. Števa has not been conscripted, and returns to the mill, very drunk, with a crowd of villagers.

The Kostelnička (soprano), or Sexton's widow, who is Jenufa's stepmother, threatens to forbid the marriage between Jenufa and Števa if he does not reform his ways. Laca, jealous of his stepbrother, who loves Jenufa only for her rosy-cheeked beauty, slashes the girl's face with his knife—a deed he instantly repents.

ACT 2. Hidden by the Kostelnička in her house, Jenufa has given birth to a boy. Despite the pleading of the Kostelnička, Števa refuses to marry Jenufa now that her face is scarred. While Jenufa is asleep, Laca comes to ask for news of her and the Kostelnička tells him about Jenufa's baby but asserts that it has died, so Jenufa is free to marry him. When Laca has gone, Kostelnička takes the baby from its cradle and goes out to drown it in the stream. Jenufa, waking, misses her son but imagines that Kostelnička has taken him to the mill. When Kostelnička returns, she persuades Jenufa that she has been ill for several days and that her baby died during that time. Laca returns and Jenufa accepts his offer of marriage.

ACT 3. On the morning of the wedding, Laca is reconciled to Števa, who intends to marry Karolka (soprano), the mayor's daughter. Kostelnička has been ill—her conscience torments her—but she blesses Jenufa and Laca, who are about to go to church when Jano (soprano), a shepherd boy, brings news that the body of a baby has been discovered in the melting ice of the stream. Jenufa admits that it is her baby and the villagers are about to attack her when Kostelnička stops them, confessing that she was the murderess. She is led away, and Jenufa finds the magnanimity to forgive her stepmother. Jenufa and Laca look forward to their new life together.

Katya Kabanova, opera in three acts with text by the composer after Ostrovsky's play *The Storm*. First produced on 23 November 1921 at Brno. Set in a small town on the banks of the River Volga about 1860.

ACT 1. Katya (soprano) is married to Tikhon Kabanov (tenor), but the household is ruled by Tikhon's widowed mother Kabanicha (contralto), who bullies

Katya. When Tikhon goes to Kazan on business, Varvara (soprano), Kabanicha's ward, tries to console Katya for her unhappiness. She has acquired the key to the garden gate, without Kabanicha's knowledge, and suggests that Katya should use it to meet Boris (tenor), who loves her.

ACT 2. Outside the garden, Kudrjaš (tenor), clerk to Dikoy (bass), a rich merchant who is Boris's uncle, waits for Varvara, who soon joins him. Katya arrives to meet Boris, and they admit their mutual love.

ACT 3. Some days later, Tikhon has returned home. A severe storm breaks out and Katya, consumed by remorse for her infidelity, publicly confesses to her husband, then runs away. She wanders along the banks of the Volga, meets and says goodbye to Boris, then throws herself into the river. Tikhon blames Kabanicha for his wife's suicide.

The Cunning Little Vixen, or *Vixen Sharpears*, opera in three acts with text by the composer, first performed on 6 November 1924 at Brno.

The Forester (baritone) catches a young Vixen (soprano) and takes her home as a pet for his children. But the Vixen escapes, after killing the Hens, and sets up house in a Badger's earth after dispossessing the Badger (bass). A male Fox (soprano or tenor) courts Sharpears and they are married by the Owl (contralto).

The Forester baits a trap with a dead hare discovered by Harašta (bass), the Poacher, near the foxes' earth. Sharpears and her now numerous family merely laugh at the trap, but Harašta returns and, more by luck than skill, shoots the Vixen. In the village inn the Forester learns from the Schoolmaster (tenor) that Harašta is getting married that day and that his bride, Terinka, has a new muff. On his way home the Forester sees a young Vixen—it is the daughter of Sharpears. He meditates on the never-ending cycle of life in the forest.

The Makropulos Case, opera in three acts with text by

the composer based on a play by Karel Čapek. First performed on 18 December 1926 at Brno. Set in contemporary Prague.

ACT 1. Judgement on a century-old lawsuit, Gregor v. Prus, is being given in court. Albert Gregor (tenor) hears from his lawyer Dr Kolenatý (bass-baritone) that he has lost the case, but Emilia Marty (soprano), a famous singer, offers information about a will in a locked cupboard in the house of Baron Prus (baritone) that could upset the judgement.

ACT 2. On stage after the opera, Prus tells Emilia Marty that another document—in Greek—is in the same drawer as the will that might prove Gregor heir to a large fortune, and also some passionate love-letters written to his ancestor, Baron Prus, signed 'E.M.'. When Prus refuses to give her the Greek document, Emilia tries to force the Baron's son Janek (tenor) to steal it for her. Finally she agrees to sleep with the Baron in return for the document.

ACT 3. In Emilia's hotel bedroom, Prus is dressing, disappointed at her coldness and total lack of response. He gives her the document. A message arrives that Janek, hopelessly in love with Emilia, has committed suicide. Gregor, Kolenatý, his clerk Vítek (tenor) and Vítek's daughter Kristina (mezzo-soprano), who was engaged to Janek, arrive. They accuse Emilia of forgery: her autograph on a photograph for Kristina and the writing on the sealed packet found in Prus's cupboard are the same. Emilia denies forgery and, fortified by some whisky, tells her story. Her real name is Elina Makropulos; she is Greek and over 300 years old. Her father, court physician to the Emperor Rudolph, invented an elixir of everlasting life which the Emperor made him try on Elina. Since then she has had many names, including Ellian Macgregor, the mistress of Baron Prus's ancestor and great-grandmother to Gregor himself. She has been frantic to retrieve the Greek document, the secret of the elixir, but now she no longer wants it. Death no longer frightens her. She offers the secret to Kristina, who burns it unopened, and Elina Makropulos at last dies.

From the House of the Dead, opera in three acts, with text by the composer adapted from the novel by Dostoievsky. Set in a Siberian prison camp and based on the writer's own experiences. First performed on 12 April 1930 at Brno.

Korngold, Erich (1897–1957), Austrian composer. His first two one-act operas, *Der Ring des Polykrates* and *Violanta*, were produced at Munich in 1916 when the composer was only 19 years old. *Die tote Stadt* (The Dead City), with text by the composer and his father, the critic Julius Korngold, under the pseudonym 'Paul Schott', was derived from Georges Rodenbach's novel *Bruges-la-morte*. It was first performed on 4 December 1920 at both Hamburg and Cologne, scoring a great popular hit. In the dead city of Bruges, Paul (tenor) mourns the death of his young wife, Marie. He sees her image in Marietta (soprano), a dancer. When Marietta profanes his wife's shrine, Paul dreams that he strangles her with Marie's long golden braid of hair.

Krenek, Ernst (born 1900), Austrian, later naturalized American, composer. The seven operas he wrote before emigrating to the USA in 1937 included *Zwingburg*, produced in 1924 in Berlin, *Leben des Orest* (The Life of Orestes), produced in 1930 in Leipzig, and *Karl V*, produced in 1937 in Prague. His post-war operas include *Pallas Athene weint* (Pallas Athene Wept) and *Der goldene Bock* (The Golden Ram), performed in 1955 and 1964 respectively, at Hamburg. But Krenek's best-known opera is undoubtedly *Jonny spielt auf* (Jonny

Strikes Up), a jazz opera with text by the composer. It was first performed 10 February 1927 at Leipzig and caused riots throughout Germany until it was banned by the Nazis. Jonny (baritone), a dance-band leader, steals a priceless violin from Daniello (baritone) and becomes the most famous violinist in the world.

Lalo, Édouard (1823–92), French composer. He wrote three operas, of which the last was unfinished at his death. Only *Le Roi d'Ys*, with text by E. Blau, first performed on 7 May 1888 at the Opéra-Comique, Paris, was successful. Margared (mezzo-soprano), daughter of the King of Ys in Brittany (bass), loves Mylio (tenor) but is betrothed to Karnac (baritone), leader of a rival kingdom. Mylio, however, loves Rozenn (soprano), Margared's sister. After he has defeated Karnac in renewed hostilities, Mylio claims Rozenn as his bride. Margared, mad with jealousy, helps Karnac open the floodgates, with the intention of drowning the town. Repenting of her action, she throws herself in the sea and Saint Corentin (bass) allows the floodwaters to subside.

Leoncavallo, Ruggero (1867–1919), Italian composer. Of his 19 operas, *Pagliacci* (Clowns), the first to be produced, has been much the most popular. His version of *La Bohème*, which he adapted from Henri Murger's novel, *Scènes de la vie de Bohème,* suffered by comparison with Puccini's version, first performed a few months before Leoncavallo's was produced on 6 May 1897 at Teatro La Fenice, Venice. *Zazà* (1900), the story of a Parisian music-hall singer and her affair with a married man, was initially successful, but two grand operas on historical themes, *I Medici* (1894), the first part of a projected trilogy on the princely Florentine family, and *Der Roland von Berlin* (1904), a commission for the

German emperor, failed to please.

Pagliacci, opera in two acts with text by the composer, first performed on 21 May 1892 at Teatro dal Verme, Milan. Set in Montalto, a village in Calabria, about 1870.

ACT 1. A prologue, sung by Tonio (baritone), rings up the curtain. A group of strolling players arrives in the village. Canio (tenor) goes off to the local tavern with Beppe (tenor), after warning his wife Nedda (soprano) that he will kill her if he discovers that she is unfaithful to him. Tonio tries to kiss Nedda, but she laughs at him and chases him away with a whip. Her lover, Silvio (baritone), comes to urge her to elope with him that night after the performance. Tonio, overhearing part of their conversation, fetches Canio, already half-drunk, from the tavern. He is not in time to discover the identity of Nedda's lover.

ACT 2. The villagers assemble for the performance. Columbine (Nedda) awaits her lover Harlequin (Beppe), who serenades her. They are just sitting down to a dinner provided by the clown Taddeo (Tonio), when Columbine's husband Pagliaccio (Canio) unexpectedly returns. Now completely drunk, Canio soon drops the pretence of the play and tries to force Nedda to betray her lover. He stabs her as she tries to escape from the platform and only then does she cry out Silvio's name as she dies. Silvio rushes forward and is knifed in turn by Canio. The comedy is ended.

Lortzing, Albert (1801–61), German composer. His 13 operas, for which he provided his own texts, were very popular in their day and include several still frequently revived in Germany.

In *Zar und Zimmermann* (Tsar and Carpenter), first produced in 1837 at Leipzig, Peter the Great, disguised as Peter Michaelis, is working in a Dutch shipyard. *Der*

Wildschütz (The Poacher), first performed in 1842 at Leipzig, deals with the tribulations of a village schoolmaster who accidentally poaches a stag belonging to the Count of Elberbach, his employer. *Undine*, an adaptation of De la Motte Fouquet's tale of the water-sprite who falls in love with a human, was first performed in 1845 at Magdeburg.

Lully, Jean-Baptiste (1632–87), Italian, later naturalized French, composer. After composing more than 30 ballets for the court of Louis XIV, Lully wrote some 20 operas, nearly all with texts by Philippe Quinault. These included *Cadmus et Hermione* (1673), *Alceste* (1674), *Thésée* (1675), *Isis* (1677), *Proserpine* (1680), *Armide et Renaud* (1686) and *Achille et Polyeucte* (1687).

Marschner, Heinrich (1795–1861), German composer. His 13 or 14 operas include three that were popular at the time and also influential on subsequent German composers, including Richard Wagner. *Der Vampyr* (1828), adapted from *The Vampire,* a story by John Polidori often attributed to Byron, and *Der Templar und die Jüdin* (1829), based on Walter Scott's novel *Ivanhoe,* were first performed at Leipzig. *Hans Heiling* (1833), with text by Eduard Devrient, based on a folk legend, was produced at the Court Theatre, Berlin.

Martinu, Bohuslav (1890–1959), Czech composer. He wrote some 15 operas, including *Julietta*, or *The Dream Book*. The text for this was drawn from a play by Georges Neveux, the French surrealist, and it was first performed on 16 May 1938 at Prague. *Comedy on the Bridge* (1937) was originally written for radio and later successfully staged. *The Greek Passion*, with text by the composer (in English) adapted from the novel *Christ Recrucified* by

Nikos Kazantzakis, was first performed on 9 June 1961 at Zurich.

Martin y Soler, Vicente (1754–1806), Spanish composer. His many operas include several settings of texts by Lorenzo da Ponte. The best-known of these is *Una cosa rara* (A Rare Thing), first performed in 1786 at the Burgtheater, Vienna, and quoted by Mozart in the supper scene of *Don Giovanni*.

Mascagni, Pietro (1863–1945), Italian composer. He spent 45 years trying, in vain, to equal the success of his first opera, *Cavalleria rusticana*, which won the contest for a one-act opera organized by the publishing house of Sonzogno in 1889. *L'amico Fritz* (Friend Fritz), a charming comedy about a rich, middle-aged bachelor who falls in love with the daughter of one of his tenants, first performed on 31 October 1891 at Teatro Costanzi, Rome, has kept a toe-hold in the repertory. In *Iris* (1898), with text by Luigi Illica, also produced at the Costanzi, a Japanese girl is forced into a brothel for refusing the advances of a powerful admirer. Eventually she kills herself by drowning in a sewer. *Le maschere* (The Maskers), produced simultaneously in Rome, Milan, Genoa and Verona on 17 January 1901, scored no more than ephemeral success. *Lodoletta* (1917), an adaptation of the novel by Ouida, and *Il piccolo Marat* (1919) fared little better.

Cavalleria rusticana (Rustic Chivalry), opera in one act with text by Menasci and Targioni-Tozzetti, after the story and play by G. Verga. First performed on 17 May 1890 at Teatro Costanzi, Rome. Set in contemporary Sicily on Easter Day.

Santuzza (soprano) has been abandoned by her lover Turiddu (tenor), a soldier, who has returned to a former flame, Lola (mezzo-soprano), now married to Alfio (baritone), the village teamster. Santuzza confesses her troubles to Mamma Lucia (contralto), Turiddu's mother; she cannot join in the Easter procession to the church, but leads the hymn in the square outside. A final approach to Turiddu fails and, in a moment of jealousy, Santuzza tells Alfio that his wife has been unfaithful to him with Turiddu.

The villagers emerge from the church. Turiddu is drinking with his friends when Alfio challenges him to fight. After bidding a tearful farewell to his mother, Turiddu is killed in the duel.

Massenet, Jules (1842–1912), French composer. He obtained his first considerable success with his fifth opera, *Le Roi de Lahore*, produced in 1877 at the Paris Opéra. *Hérodiade* (1881), first performed at Brussels, was followed by *Manon* (1884), which received 2,000 performances at the Opéra-Comique in seventy years. *Le Cid* (1885), *Esclarmonde* (1889) and *Thaïs* (1894) were all well received at the Opéra. Meanwhile *Werther* (1892), premiered in Vienna and performed at the Opéra-Comique the following year, soon became Massenet's most popular work after *Manon*. *La Navarraise* (1894) was first produced at Covent Garden; *Sapho* (1897) and *Cendrillon* (1899) at the Opéra-Comique. The remaining ten of Massenet's 27 operas include *Le Jongleur de Notre-Dame* (1902), *Thérèse* (1907) and *Don Quichotte* (1910), all first performed at Monte Carlo.

Hérodiade, opera in four acts with text by P. Milliet and H. Grémont, after a story by Flaubert. First performed on 19 December 1881 at Théâtre de la Monnaie, Brussels. A version of the biblical legend of Salome (soprano) and her love for John the Baptist (tenor), whose fulminations against her mother Herodias (mezzo-soprano) and stepfather Herod (baritone) result in the prophet's death and Salome's suicide.

Manon, opera in five acts with text by H. Meilhac and P. Gille, after the Abbé Prévost's novel *Manon Lescaut*. First performed on 19 January 1884 at the Opéra-Comique, Paris. Set in eighteenth-century France.

ACT 1. Manon (soprano), who is being escorted to a convent by her cousin, Lescaut (baritone), meets the Chevalier des Grieux (tenor) at an inn in Amiens, and elopes with him in the coach of the elderly Guillot (tenor).

ACT 2. In Paris, Des Grieux and Manon have spent all their money. Lescaut and Brétigny (baritone) visit the young lovers and the latter pays court to Manon, indicating that he is rich as well as noble. Des Grieux is abducted by his father's servants.

ACT 3. Manon, now the mistress of Brétigny, attends a fête on the Cours-de-la-reine. To impress her, Guillot has arranged for the Opéra ballet to perform, but Manon leaves in the middle of the dance, having overheard the Count des Grieux (bass), the Chevalier's father, tell Brétigny that his son is about to take holy orders.

At the church of Saint-Sulpice, the Count tries in vain to dissuade his son from taking orders. Manon, when she arrives, is more successful and the couple run away together.

ACT 4. Penniless again, Manon and Des Grieux attempt to recoup their fortunes at the Hôtel de Transylvanie, a Paris gaming house. Des Grieux wins against Guillot, who accuses him of cheating. The police are called and they arrest Manon and Des Grieux.

ACT 5. On the road to Le Havre, Lescaut and the Chevalier plan to abduct Manon, who is being deported as a prostitute. They bribe the guard in charge of the female prisoners to release Manon, but she is exhausted and dies in the Chevalier's arms.

Werther, opera in four acts with text by Blau, Milliet and Hartmann, after Goethe's novel *The Sorrows of Young Werther*. First performed on 16 February 1892, at the Hofoper, Vienna. Set in Frankfurt about 1780.

ACT 1. Werther (tenor), a poet, falls in love with Charlotte (mezzo-soprano), the daughter of the Magistrate (bass). She returns his affection, but tells him that she promised her mother, now dead, to marry Albert (baritone), a friend of the family.

ACT 2. Charlotte and Albert, who have been married three months, go to church accompanied by Sophie (soprano), Charlotte's younger sister. Werther, unable to hide his unhappiness, comes to say goodbye. He will go away until Christmas.

ACT 3. At Christmas, Charlotte re-reads Werther's letters. When Werther appears she finds strength to send him away. A servant comes to borrow Albert's pistols for Werther, who is going on a long journey. Charlotte rushes out of the house.

ACT 4. In Werther's rooms Charlotte finds the poet lying wounded. She confesses her love and he dies contented.

Thaïs, opera in three acts with text by L. Gallet, based on a novel by Anatole France. First performed on 16 March 1894 at the Paris Opéra. Set in Alexandria in the fourth century. Athanaël (baritone), a Cenobite monk, goes to Alexandria with the intention of reforming Thaïs (soprano), the famous courtesan. He succeeds but, having escorted her to a convent in the desert, realizes that he has fallen in love with her. Returning to the convent, he finds she is on the point of death.

Don Quichotte, opera in five acts with text by Henri Cain taken from a play based on Cervantes' novel. First performed on 19 February 1910 at Monte Carlo.

Don Quixote (bass) has fallen in love with Dulcinea (contralto), who promises to reward his love if he retrieves a necklace of hers stolen by bandits. Accompanied by Sancho Panza (baritone), Don Quixote sets off in search of the necklace and succeeds in getting it back. When he asks Dulcinea to marry him, she explains that she is a courtesan.

In his delirium, as he lies dying, Don Quixote sees a vision of Dulcinea.

Menotti, Gian-Carlo (born 1911), American composer of Italian birth. His first opera, *Amelia Goes to the Ball* (1937), for which he wrote his own libretto (as with all his works), was produced at Philadelphia. *The Island God* (1942), first performed at the Metropolitan, New York, was followed by *The Medium* (1946), *The Telephone* (1947), *The Consul* (1950) and *Amahl and the Night Visitors* (1952), originally written for NBC Television and later staged all over the world. *The Saint of Bleecker Street* (1954) and *Maria Golovin* (1958) scored popular successes. *The Last Savage* was first performed (in French) in 1963 at the Opéra-Comique, Paris, and the following year (in English) at the Metropolitan.

The Medium, opera in two acts with text by the composer, first performed on 8 May 1946 at Columbia University. Madame Flora (contralto), a medium, her daughter Monica (soprano) and Toby, a mute, prepare for a séance. The clients, Mr and Mrs Gobineau (baritone and soprano) and Mrs Nolan (mezzo-soprano), arrive and are duly impressed by the performance, which is completely fraudulent. Suddenly Madame Flora screams—she has felt the touch of a real ghost.

The Consul, opera in three acts with text by the composer, first performed on 1 March 1950 at Philadelphia. Set in Europe after World War II.

ACT 1. For political reasons John Sorel (baritone) has to flee the country, leaving his Mother (contralto), his wife Magda (soprano) and his child behind. Magda goes to the consulate to try to obtain a visa to join her husband. In the ante-room of the consulate, presided over by the Secretary (mezzo-soprano), half a dozen other people are also waiting, including Mr Kofner (bass-baritone), Anna Gomez (soprano), Vera Boronel (contralto) and a Magician (tenor).

ACT 2. The Secret Police Agent (bass) tells Magda she would be granted a visa at once if she volunteered information on her husband's friends. She refuses. Assam (baritone), a friend of John's, brings news that he is still in the country, waiting until Magda can get a visa. The Mother discovers that Magda's child has died of starvation. In the consulate the same people are waiting. Magda asks to see the Consul, and when her request is refused she loses control and denounces the cruelty and injustice of the system.

ACT 3. Magda is still waiting to see the Consul. Assam comes in to say that John intends to return, having heard of the death of his child. The Secretary is just closing the office when John Sorel arrives, asking for Magda. The Secret Police Agent follows him in and arrests him, despite the Secretary's protests. As Sorel is taken away, the Secretary dials a telephone number.

In the Sorel apartment the telephone rings, but it has stopped by the time that Magda comes in. She turns on the gas and prepares to kill herself. The telephone rings again, but it is too late, and Magda dies.

Meyerbeer, Giacomo (1791–1864), German composer. Three early operas with German texts were performed in various German cities. Meyerbeer then composed six operas for Italian theatres, the last of which, *Il crociato in Egitto* (The Crusader in Egypt), was performed with huge success at the Teatro Fenice, Venice, in 1824 and at the Théâtre-Italien, Paris, the following year. *Robert le diable* (1831), Meyerbeer's first setting of a French text, was followed by *Les Huguenots*

(1836), *Le Prophète* (1849) and, posthumously, *L'Africaine* (1865), all produced with spectacular effect at the Paris Opéra. *Ein Feldlager in Schlesien* (1844), first performed at Berlin, was later entirely rewritten and, as *L'Étoile du nord* (1854), produced at the Opéra-Comique, where *Le Pardon de Ploërmel* (1859), or *Dinorah*, was also performed.

Montemezzi, Italo (1875–1952), Italian composer. The first of his operas to be performed, *Giovanni Gallurese* (1905) and *Hellera* (1909), were given at Turin. *L'amore dei tre re* (1913), the work by which he is now remembered, was produced at La Scala, Milan, as were *La nave* (1918) and *La notte de Zoraima* (1931).

L'amore dei tre re (The Love of Three Kings), opera in three acts with text by Sem Benelli, first performed on 10 April 1913 at La Scala, Milan. Set in tenth-century Italy. Fiora (soprano), once betrothed to Avito (tenor), former Prince of Altura, has been forced to marry Manfredo (baritone), son of King Archibaldo (bass), who conquered Altura many years before. In her husband's absence Fiora becomes Avito's lover. The old King suspects her but, being blind, can prove nothing. When she refuses to divulge the name of her lover he strangles her. Fiora is laid on a bier. Avito comes to kiss her for the last time and dies from poison with which Archibaldo has anointed her lips. Manfredo, too, kisses her and dies. The King discovers he has killed the son whom he loves.

Monteverdi, Claudio (1567–1643), Italian composer. The music for many of his operas is lost, but three masterpieces remain to represent the first great operatic composer in the current repertory.

La favola d'Orfeo (The Legend of Orpheus), opera in prologue and five acts, with text by A. Striggio, first publicly performed on 24 February 1607 at the Court Theatre, Mantua. Nymphs and shepherds celebrate the wedding of Orpheus (tenor) and Eurydice (soprano), who goes to pick flowers with her companions. A Messenger (mezzo-soprano) brings news of the death of Eurydice, who has been bitten by a snake. Orpheus laments his bride, then descends to the Underworld to attempt to get her back. His singing charms Charon into giving him passage across the River Styx. Proserpina (soprano) prevails upon Pluto (bass) to return Eurydice to life. Orpheus, looking back to see that Eurydice is following, breaks the condition of her freedom, and Eurydice falls dead once more. Back on earth Orpheus laments his loss until Apollo (tenor), his father, translates him to immortality.

Il ritorno d'Ulisse in patria (The Return Home of Ulysses), opera in prologue and five acts with text by G. Badoaro, first performed at the Teatro San Cassiano, Venice, in 1641.

Penelope (mezzo-soprano) laments the continued absence of her husband, Ulysses, after the end of the Trojan War. Ulysses (baritone) is shipwrecked on the coast of Ithaca and sheltered by the old swineherd Eumetes (tenor), who does not at first recognize his master. Assisted by Minerva (soprano), Ulysses' son Telemachus (tenor) is reunited with his father. In the palace, Penelope's suitors are feasting. They mock the beggar brought in by Eumetes. None of the suitors succeeds in drawing the bow of Ulysses until the beggar steps forward and draws it with ease, killing the suitors. Penelope at first refuses to recognize her husband, despite the assurances of Telemachus and of the old nurse Ericlea (mezzo-soprano). At last Ulysses himself convinces her.

L'incoronazione di Poppea (The Coronation of Poppaea), opera in prologue and three acts, with text by

G. F. Busanello, derived from Tacitus' *Annals*. First performed in 1652 at the Teatro Santi Giovanni e Paolo, Venice. Set in Rome about AD 55.

Because of his love for Poppaea (soprano), the Emperor Nero (tenor or soprano) wishes to divorce his wife Octavia (mezzo-soprano). When Seneca (bass), his former tutor, objects, Nero orders him to take his own life. Octavia seeks the aid of Ottone (baritone or soprano), Poppaea's former lover, and demands that he should kill Poppaea. Ottone, dressed in the clothes of Drusilla (soprano), Octavia's lady-in-waiting, who loves him, enters the room where Poppaea lies asleep, intending to stab her. The Goddess of Love (soprano) wakens Arnalta (contralto or tenor), Poppaea's nurse, who chases away the intruder. Drusilla is arrested and claims to have made the attack, but Ottone confesses. He is banished and Drusilla pleads to go with him into exile. Octavia is also banished, and Nero and Poppaea celebrate their marriage, expressing their love for each other.

Mozart, Wolfgang Amadeus (1756–91), Austrian composer. Mozart was only eleven years old when his first two operatic efforts were performed at Salzburg. The following year he composed two more, *La finta semplice* (The Feigned Simpleton) and *Bastien und Bastienne*. *Mitridate, re di Ponto* (1770), *Ascanio in Alba* (1771) and *Lucio Silla* (1772) were first performed at the Teatro Regio Ducale, Milan; *Il sogno di Scipione* (1772) and *Il re pastore* (1775) in Salzburg; and *La finta giardiniera*, or The False Gardener-girl (1775) in Munich. *Zaide*, *L'oca del Cairo* and *Lo sposo deluso* were uncompleted. The one-act *Der Schauspieldirektor*, or The Impresario (1786) was given at Schönbrunn Palace near Vienna. Meanwhile, the seven great operas of Mozart's maturity were inaugurated with *Idomeneo*.

Idomeneo, re di Creta, opera in three acts with text by G. B. Varesco, first performed on 29 January 1781 at the Residenztheater, Munich. Set in Crete at the end of the Trojan War.

ACT 1. The imminent return home of Idomeneo, King of Crete (tenor), is occasion for the release of Trojan prisoners, including Ilia (soprano), daughter of King Priam. She loves, and is loved by, Idamante (soprano or tenor), Idomeneo's son, who is also loved by Elettra (soprano), the Greek princess. Rejoicings are cut short by the news that the fleet carrying Idomeneo and his men has been wrecked.

Idomeneo, safely washed ashore, in gratitude promises to sacrifice the first person he meets to Neptune. He is horrified when that person turns out to be Idamante, who cannot understand why his father greets him so strangely.

ACT 2. In an attempt to evade his vow, Idomeneo arranges for Idamante to marry Elettra and escort her back to Greece, though he realizes that Idamante and Ilia love each other.

ACT 3. Neptune sends a monster to ravage Crete, and Idomeneo is forced to acknowledge his unfulfilled promise of sacrifice. Idamante slays the monster, then offers himself willingly as victim. Ilia then offers herself in place of Idamante, whereupon the Voice of Neptune (bass) announces that Idomeneo should hand over his crown to Idamante and Ilia, thus fulfilling his vow. There is general rejoicing, except on the part of Elettra.

Die Entführung aus dem Serail (The Abduction from the Seraglio), opera in three acts with text by G. Stephanie, first performed on 16 July 1782 at the Burgtheater, Vienna. Set in eighteenth-century Turkey.

Belmonte (tenor), a Spanish nobleman, has traced his beloved Constanze (soprano), her English maid Blonde (soprano) and his servant Pedrillo (tenor), who were abducted by pirates, to the house of the Pasha Selim (speaking role). Belmonte gains entry to the house—though not, of course, to the harem—by pretending that he is a famous architect. He is horrified to learn from Pedrillo that the Pasha wishes to marry Constanze, though she has so far resisted all his threats and entreaties. Pedrillo is more worried by the fact that Blonde has been given as personal slave to Osmin (bass), the harem overseer, but she, with her English love of freedom, is perfectly capable of taking care of herself. Pedrillo makes Osmin drunk, so that Belmonte and Constanze can meet. The two men plan to rescue the two women that night, and escape in Belmonte's ship. The plan is thwarted when a ladder for gaining access to the harem is discovered. Osmin and his guards quickly recapture the four Europeans. Pasha Selim discovers that Belmonte is the son of the man responsible for his own exile, but to demonstrate his magnanimity he allows them all to leave, to the fury of Osmin, who is deprived of his Blonde.

Le nozze di Figaro (The Marriage of Figaro), opera in four acts with text by Lorenzo da Ponte after the play by Beaumarchais. First performed on 1 May 1786 at the Burgtheater, Vienna. Set in eighteenth-century Seville. The libretto sticks closely to Beaumarchais, though many of the more revolutionary sentiments have been removed or toned down.

ACT 1. Susanna (soprano), maid to Countess Almaviva, and Figaro (baritone), the Count's valet, are getting married. The Count (baritone), who has designs himself on Susanna, opposes the marriage, ostensibly on behalf of Marcellina (soprano), his wife's ex-governess, to whom Figaro once proposed marriage as security for some money owed her. Cherubino (soprano), a young page, overhears the Count making advances to Susanna, and is sent to join the Count's regiment. When the time comes for the betrothal ceremony, the Count postpones it.

ACT 2. In her room, the Countess regrets the loss of her husband's love. Figaro, Susanna and the Countess plan to dress Cherubino as a girl and send 'her' to a rendezvous with the Count in place of Susanna. The Count, supposedly out hunting, returns unexpectedly to find his wife's door locked. Cherubino hides in a dressing-room, whose door-key the Countess refuses to surrender to the Count. While he, accompanied by his wife, is out of the room fetching tools to break down the door, Susanna takes the page's place in the dressing-room while Cherubino jumps out of the window. The Countess gives the key to her husband, confessing that it is Cherubino inside; they were planning a harmless charade for that evening. When the door is opened and Susanna steps out, Count and Countess are equally surprised. Figaro arrives, hoping that the wedding may now proceed, but Antonio (bass), the gardener, complains that someone has jumped out of the window on to his flowers. Figaro claims that it was he who jumped. Marcellina enters, accompanied by Doctor Bartolo (bass), the Countess's former guardian, and Don Basilio (tenor), music master and go-between. The Count decides that Marcellina's claim must be legally examined.

ACT 3. The Count is aware that something he does not quite understand is going on in his household. Susanna comes to borrow his smelling salts for her mistress and promises him an assignation for that evening. Don Curzio (tenor), the lawyer, gives judgement on Marcellina's claim: Figaro must pay her or marry her. However, it transpires that Figaro is the long-lost son of Marcellina and Bartolo. Susanna arrives with money from the Countess to pay off Figaro's debt and is upset to find him embracing Marcellina, but the situation is soon made clear to her and a double wedding is planned.

The Countess dictates a letter for Susanna to write to the Count, making an assignation for that evening—an assignation that the Countess means to keep herself. The girls of the estate, led by Barbarina (soprano), bring flowers to the Countess, who particularly admires one modest maiden—Cherubino in disguise. During the ceremony, Susanna hands the note of assignation to the Count, who pricks his finger on the pin sealing it, as Figaro notices. The celebrations continue with dancing.

ACT 4. In the garden Barbarina is searching for the pin, which the Count gave her to return to Susanna. Figaro realizes that the note must have been written by his bride, and pours out his bitterness at women's infidelity. The Countess, dressed in Susanna's clothes, meets the Count as promised, but they are disturbed by Cherubino. Susanna, dressed in the Countess's clothes, does not deceive Figaro for long and, as they hear the Count returning in search of 'Susanna', he begins to make passionate love to the 'Countess'. The Count calls for lights and publicly denounces his wife and Figaro. The 'Countess' begs for forgiveness, which he refuses until the voice of the real Countess is heard, joining in the plea. It is the Count's turn to beg for forgiveness, which he is granted, and the celebrations recommence.

Don Giovanni (originally *Il dissoluto punito*, or The Libertine Punished), opera in two acts with text by L. da Ponte, first performed on 29 October 1787 at Prague. Set in Seville in the seventeenth century.

ACT 1. While his servant Leporello (bass) keeps guard, Don Giovanni (baritone) attempts to seduce Donna Anna (soprano). The noise brings out the Commendatore (bass), Anna's father, who challenges the seducer while Anna runs for help. Giovanni kills the old man and disappears with Leporello before Anna returns with Don Ottavio (tenor), her betrothed. She makes him swear to avenge her father's death.

Giovanni overhears a woman railing against a lover who has deserted her. It is Donna Elvira (soprano), whom he himself seduced in Burgos. Leaving Leporello to show Elvira the catalogue of his conquests—1,003 in Spain alone—he escapes.

Zerlina (soprano), a country girl, and Masetto (baritone) are celebrating their betrothal with a group of friends. Giovanni invites them all to his house, contriving to remain alone with Zerlina, but his amorous intentions are thwarted by the arrival of Elvira. Anna and Ottavio enlist Giovanni's aid in their search for the Commendatore's murderer. After Elvira has again interrupted with warnings about Giovanni's character, Anna recognizes his voice, as he says goodbye, as that of the assassin. She relates the details of her experience to Ottavio, who at first is loath to believe that Giovanni is guilty, but Anna persuades him.

Giovanni is holding a party. Masetto berates Zerlina for abandoning him that morning, but she calms him down. Three masqueraders arrive and are invited to the party by Leporello. They are Elvira, Anna and Ottavio, who swear solemn vengeance on the profligate. Inside the house, dancing is going on. Giovanni arranges to take Zerlina into another room. Her screams interrupt the entertainment and, though Giovanni tries to put the blame on Leporello, the masqueraders reveal their identities and denounce him.

ACT 2. Don Giovanni has designs on Elvira's maid, so he exchanges clothes with Leporello and, after luring Elvira down from her balcony, sends Leporello off with her. He sings a serenade under the window, but is then disturbed by Masetto, who takes him for Leporello, and his friends, who are searching for Giovanni. Having deprived Masetto of his pistol, Giovanni beats him up and escapes. Zerlina, hearing Masetto's groans, comforts him.

Meanwhile Leporello is trying to get rid of Elvira. They are surprised first by Anna and Ottavio, then by Zerlina and Masetto, who all denounce the supposed villain. Elvira pleads for his life until he is revealed as Leporello, and manages to escape. Ottavio, now certain that Giovanni is the Commendatore's murderer, announces his intention of informing the authorities.

Giovanni and Leporello meet in the churchyard. Giovanni notices a newly erected statue of the Commendatore and forces Leporello to ask the Statue to dinner. The Statue accepts with a nod.

Giovanni is eating his supper, entertained by musicians who play tunes from popular operas (including *The Marriage of Figaro*). Elvira makes a final attempt to get Giovanni to repent, but he laughs at her. The Statue arrives, to the sound of tremendous footsteps. Leporello, petrified, hides. In his turn the Statue asks Giovanni to supper with him. The unrepentant libertine agrees, and is dragged down to Hell by demons. The other characters hurry in to find Leporello cowering under the table. He tries to explain what has happened. Leporello has to find a new master. Elvira will enter a convent, and Anna begs Ottavio for a year in which to recover from her father's death before their marriage.

Cosi fan tutte (literally, So Do All Women), opera in two acts with text by L. da Ponte, first performed on 26 January 1790 at the Burgtheater, Vienna. Set in contemporary Naples.

ACT 1. Two young officers, Guglielmo (baritone) and Ferrando (tenor), boast that their respective mistresses, Fiordiligi (soprano) and her sister Dorabella (mezzo-soprano), are faithful. Don Alfonso (baritone), an elderly cynic, bets that he can prove the young men wrong within a day. They agree to obey his instructions.

The officers, accompanied by Alfonso, say goodbye to the sisters, pretending that they are being sent on active service. The girls are heartbroken. Alfonso enlists the aid of Despina, their maid (soprano), who thinks one man is as good as another. Disguised as Albanians, Ferrando and Guglielmo pay ardent court to the sisters, but Fiordiligi and Dorabella stand firm. They are in the garden when the Albanians drink poison and collapse. A doctor is summoned (Despina in disguise) who cures the moribund Albanians with a magnet.

ACT 2. The Albanians serenade the two girls, who pair off with opposite partners from their original ones. Dorabella quickly succumbs to the disguised Guglielmo but Fiordiligi resists Ferrando, though attracted to him. She decides to join her lover on the battlefield but Ferrando appears at her side again, and this time she admits her love. Alfonso, having won his bet, advises a double wedding. The sisters have just signed the contracts before a notary (Despina again), when the officers are heard returning. The Albanians rush out and come back in their proper guise. Alfonso carefully brings the signed contracts to their notice. The 'notary' is found, and also the Albanians' clothes. The sisters blame Alfonso for everything that has happened.

Die Zauberflöte (The Magic Flute), opera in two acts with text by E. Schikaneder, first performed on 30 September 1791, at the Theater auf der Wieden, Vienna.

ACT 1. Tamino (tenor), an Egyptian prince, is pursued by a huge snake. When he falls unconscious, three Ladies (two sopranos and mezzo-soprano) kill the serpent. Papageno (baritone), a bird-catcher, boasts to Tamino that he killed the serpent, and is rebuked by the Ladies. They show Tamino a portrait of Pamina (soprano), daughter to the Queen of Night (soprano), whom they serve. Pamina has been abducted by Sarastro (bass), the High Priest of Isis and Osiris. The Queen herself appears to encourage Tamino to rescue her daughter. The Ladies give Tamino a magic flute and Papageno, who is to accompany him, a set of magic bells.

Pamina tries to escape, but the Moor, Monostatos (tenor), recaptures her. Monostatos and Papageno each think the other the devil, but the latter, recognizing Pamina from the portrait he carries, sets her free. Tamino, led by three Genii (womens' or boys' voices), arrives in front of the temples of Wisdom, Reason and Nature. From one emerges a Speaker (baritone), who informs Tamino that Sarastro, far from being the tyrant described by the Queen of Night, is wise and benevolent. Tamino plays his flute and wild animals flock to hear it. Papageno and Pamina also hear the flute but miss Tamino. Instead they are confronted with Monostatos and his men, but Papageno's magic bells send the slaves dancing harmlessly away. Sarastro enters with his priests and followers, and Pamina explains that she escaped only to avoid the Moor's unwelcome attentions. Monostatos brings in Tamino and is rewarded, not with praise but with punishment. Tamino and Pamina greet each other joyfully, but they must undergo severe ordeals before they can be united.

ACT 2. Sarastro tells the priests of his plans for Tamino and Pamina, and prays to Isis and Osiris for strength on their behalf.

Tamino and a reluctant Papageno are ordered to keep silent. The three Ladies accuse Tamino of betraying their Queen. He does not answer and stops Papageno from doing so.

Pamina lies asleep in the garden. Monostatos gloats over her beauty. His evil intentions are thwarted by the Queen of Night who gives her daughter a dagger, ordering her to kill Sarastro with it. Monostatos threatens to tell Sarastro if Pamina will not give herself to him, but the High Priest assures Pamina that revenge, even on her mother, is not his way of dealing with evil-doers.

Tamino and Papageno are still under orders to keep silent, but the latter talks to an old woman who claims to be his promised sweetheart, Papagena. The magic flute and bells are returned, and Tamino plays his flute. The sound brings Pamina running, and she cannot understand why Tamino will not speak to her.

Priests sing in praise of Isis and Osiris. Sarastro tells Tamino and Pamina to bid each other a last farewell.

Papageno still longs for his sweetheart. The old woman appears again, and this time reveals herself as a charming young woman under the disguise, before she is whisked away.

The three Genii prevent Pamina from killing herself with her mother's dagger. Tamino is to undergo the trials of Fire and Water. This time Pamina is allowed to accompany him, and to the sound of the flute they pass safely through.

Papageno, unable to find his Papagena, decides to hang himself. The Genii advise him to play the magic bells instead, and she appears.

The Queen, her Ladies and Monostatos plan to blow up Sarastro's temple but light triumphs over darkness, and Tamino and Pamina, having passed their trials, are united by Sarastro.

La clemenza di Tito, opera in two acts with text by Metastasio, revised by Mazzola. First performed on 6 December 1791 at Prague. Set in Rome in AD 80.

ACT 1. The Emperor Titus (tenor) plans to marry Servilia (soprano), the sister of his friend Sextus (soprano), but Servilia is in love with Annius (soprano). Titus transfers his attentions to Vitellia (soprano), daughter of the late Emperor Vitellius, but she, insulted that he had not chosen her in the first place, has persuaded Sextus, who is in love with her, to kill Titus. The Capitol is set ablaze and Sextus stabs a man he takes to be the Emperor, but who is in fact one of the conspirators.

ACT 2. Publius (bass), Commander of the Praetorian Guard, arrests Sextus and the Senate finds him guilty. Titus at first cannot believe in his friend's guilt, but Sextus offers no explanation and is sentenced to death. Vitellia resolves to confess that she instigated the plot, and does so, but Titus has already decided to exercise his clemency and pardons both Sextus and Vitellia.

Musgrave, Thea (born 1929), Scottish composer. Her operas include *The Abbot of Drimock* (1958), first performed in concert; *The Decision* (1967), produced by the New Opera Company at Sadler's Wells; *The Voice of Ariadne* (1973), first performed by the English Opera Group at Aldeburgh; and *Mary, Queen of Scots* (1977), first performed by Scottish Opera at the Edinburgh Festival.

Mussorgsky, Modest Petrovich (1839–81), Russian composer. Of his five operas, only *Boris Godunov* (1874) was finished by the composer. *Khovanshchina*, completed and scored by Rimsky-Korsakov, was first performed in 1886 at St Petersburg, and *Sorochintsy Fair* has been completed in several different versions.

Boris Godunov, opera originally in seven scenes, with text by the composer taken mainly from Pushkin's play. First performed (prologue and four acts) on 8 February 1874 at the Maryinsky Theatre, St Petersburg; rescored by Rimsky-Korsakov, 1896, at St Petersburg; second version rescored by Rimsky-Korsakov, 9 May 1908, at the Paris Opéra; original version, 1928, at Leningrad. Set in Poland and Russia between 1598 and 1605.

PROLOGUE. The people urge Boris Godunov to accept the crown of Russia. Boris (bass) accepts and is crowned tsar in Moscow.

ACT 1. In the monastery of Chudov, the old monk Pimen (bass) is finishing his chronicle of Russian history. Grigori (tenor), a young monk, questions him about the Tsarevich Dimitri, murdered as a child by Boris.

At an inn near the Lithuanian border, Grigori, travelling with two vagabond monks, Vaarlam (bass) and Missail (tenor), questions the Hostess (mezzo-soprano) on the route across the border. When the police arrive in search of him he jumps from the window.

ACT 2. In the Kremlin, Boris's son Fyodor (mezzo-soprano) and the Nurse (contralto) try to divert the Tsarevna Xenia (soprano), whose intended husband has died. The Tsar enters and, after hearing his son's geography lesson, expresses the torment that his conscience causes him. Prince Shuisky (tenor) warns Boris that a pretender calling himself Dimitri (the former monk Grigori) has been acclaimed tsar in Poland. He reassures the Tsar that the murdered child was indeed Dimitri. Left alone, Boris becomes hysterical as a chiming clock begins to strike and he takes the moving figure as the ghost of the dead Tsarevich.

ACT 3. Marina Minishek (soprano), a Polish princess, hopes to marry Dimitri and become Empress of Russia. The Jesuit, Rangoni (bass), reminds her that her first duty is to convert the Russians to the true faith. In the garden, Dimitri waits for Marina, with whom he is in love. At first she rejects his suit, but when he says that he will march on Moscow at the head of an army, she succumbs to his passionate wooing.

ACT 4. In the Kremlin, Prince Shuisky tells the boyars how Boris seemed troubled by some ghost or evil spirit. When the Tsar enters, Shuisky suggests that he should hear an aged monk who wishes to speak to him. Pimen is brought in and relates the miracle of a blind man who was cured by a visit to the tomb of the murdered Tsarevich Dimitri. Boris faints and, when he recovers, sends for his son. Left alone with Fyodor, he gives the boy his final instructions as heir to the throne of Russia. The boyars return and Boris falls dead.

In the forest of Kromy the people wait to welcome Dimitri, who arrives at the head of his army and then leads the crowd toward Moscow. An Idiot (tenor) laments the hard lot of the people of Russia.

Nicolai, Otto (1810–49), German composer. His early operas, composed to Italian texts, included *Il templario* (1840), an adaptation of Walter Scott's novel *Ivanhoe*, first produced at Turin. His most successful opera, *Die lustigen Weiber von Windsor*, with text derived from Shakespeare's comedy *The Merry Wives of Windsor*, was first performed on 9 March 1849 at the Court Theatre, Berlin, only two months before the composer's death.

Nielsen, Carl (1865–1931), Danish composer. He wrote two operas, *Saul and David* (1902) and *Masquerade* (1906), a comedy still popular in Denmark today.

Offenbach, Jacques (1819–80), French composer of German origin. After a lifetime spent in producing enormously successful light operas or operettas such as *Orphée aux enfers*, or Orpheus in the Underworld (1858), *La Belle Hélène* (1864), *La Vie parisienne* (1867), *La Grande Duchesse de Gérolstein* (1867) and *La Périchole* (1868), Offenbach wrote one serious opera, *Les Contes d'Hoffmann*, which was not finished at the time of his death.

Les Contes d'Hoffmann (The Tales of Hoffmann), opera

in three acts with text by Jules Barbier based on a play by Barbier and Michel Carré, itself derived from three stories by E. T. A. Hoffmann. First performed on 10 February 1881 at the Opéra-Comique, Paris.

PROLOGUE. During the interval of *Don Giovanni* at the opera house in Nuremberg, students drink in Luther's tavern next door. Hoffmann (tenor), a poet, and his friend Niklausse (mezzo-soprano) join them and Hoffmann is persuaded to recount the stories of his three tragic loves.

ACT 1. In the first episode Hoffmann is in love with Olympia (soprano), so-called daughter of Spalanzani (tenor), an inventor. Guests arrive and Olympia entertains them with a song. Then Hoffmann, wearing spectacles provided by the scientist Coppelius (baritone), dances with the girl, but falls exhausted by her non-stop gyrations. Coppelius, whom Spalanzani has cheated, pulls Olympia limb from limb—she was only a mechanical doll.

ACT 2. Hoffmann's second love is Antonia (soprano), daughter of Councillor Crespel (baritone) of Munich. Like her dead mother, she is a singer, but has also inherited the consumption that killed her mother and is forbidden to sing. Dr Miracle (baritone), whom Crespel holds responsible for his wife's death, insists on treating Antonia and she, with the Voice of her Mother (mezzo-soprano) in her ears to encourage her, sings until she collapses. Crespel blames Hoffmann for his daughter's death.

ACT 3. The third episode takes place in Venice. Hoffmann is now enamoured of the courtesan Giulietta (soprano), who is bribed with a diamond by a sorcerer, Dapertutto (baritone), to obtain Hoffmann's reflection for him, just as she obtained that of her lover Schlemil (bass). Hoffmann kills Schlemil to get the key to Giulietta's bedroom, but she has already gone off with

Pittichinaccio (tenor), another admirer.

EPILOGUE. Back in Luther's tavern, Hoffmann is completely drunk. The opera is over and Stella (soprano), the prima donna and incarnation of Hoffmann's three loves, comes to find him, but he ignores her. She goes off with Councillor Lindorf (bass), Hoffmann's evil genius, while the Muse (spoken role, or in some versions Nicklausse transformed) claims the poet Hoffmann as her own.

Orff, Carl (1895–1982), German composer. After *Carmina Burana* (1937), a scenic cantata using a Latin text, he wrote both words and music for *Der Mond* (The Moon), produced in 1939 at Munich, and *Die Kluge* (The Clever Girl), based on a tale by the Brothers Grimm, performed in 1943 at Frankfurt. *Catulli Carmina* (1943) and *Trionfi dell'Afrodite* (1953) completed the trilogy of works to Latin texts begun with *Carmina Burana*. *Antigonae* (1949), adapted from Sophocles, was produced at Salzburg.

Paisiello, Giovanni (1740–1816), Italian composer. A prolific composer, he wrote nearly 100 operas, both serious and comic, the best-known of which, *Il barbiere di Siviglia* (The Barber of Seville), an adaptation of the play by Beaumarchais, was first performed on 26 September 1782 in St Petersburg. It held its popularity for more than 30 years until it was eclipsed by Rossini's version.

Pepusch, John Christopher (1667–1752), English composer of German birth. His claim to fame rests solely on his arrangement of music for *The Beggar's Opera*, a ballad opera with text by John Gay, first performed on 29 January 1728 at Lincoln's Inn Fields Theatre, London. Macheath (baritone), the highwayman, is loved by both Polly (soprano), daughter of the fence Peachum (bass), and Lucy (soprano), daughter of Lockit (baritone), jailer of Newgate prison. Macheath is condemned to be hanged, but is reprieved at the last minute.

Pergolesi, Giovanni Battista (1710–36), Italian composer. His operas include *Il prigionier superbo*, a serious opera first performed on 28 August 1733 at the Teatro San Bartolomeo, Naples, that embraced the comic intermezzo *La serva padrona* (The Maid Mistress), which became popular throughout Europe on its own. Serpina (soprano) tricks her employer Uberto (bass) into marrying her by dressing up Vespone (silent role), her fellow servant, as his rival.

Pfitzner, Hans (1869–1949), German composer. He wrote five operas of which *Palestrina*, in three acts with text by the composer, first performed on 12 June 1917 at the Prinzregententheater, Munich, is the best-known.

ACT 1. Palestrina (tenor), the sixteenth-century Roman composer, is asked by Cardinal Borromeo (baritone) to write a mass as a model to convince Pope Pius IV of the viability of contemporary church music. Palestrina refuses, feeling too old and tired. He falls asleep and sees a vision of his dead wife Lucretia, while angelic voices dictate the mass to him.

ACT 2. At the Council of Trent, now in its eighteenth and last year, the delegates from various countries argue until Morone (baritone), the papal legate, brings the session to an end.

ACT 3. In Rome, Palestrina's mass is being sung at the Pope's palace, but the composer has been ill. The Pope comes to congratulate Palestrina on the success of the mass, while Cardinal Borromeo falls on his knees before his old friend.

Ponchielli, Amilcare (1834–86), Italian composer. His first opera, *I promessi sposi* (1856), was based on Manzoni's novel *The Betrothed*. *La Gioconda*, with text by 'Tobia Gorrio' (Arrigo Boito), first performed on 8 April 1876 at La Scala, Milan, with great popular success, is the only one of his operas still in the current repertory.

Gioconda, a Venetian ballad-singer, is in love with Enzo Grimaldo (tenor), a proscribed Genoese nobleman, but she loves Laura (mezzo-soprano), wife of Alvise Badoero (bass), head of the State Inquisition. Because Laura interceded with Alvise on behalf of La Cieca (contralto), Gioconda's blind mother, Gioconda bribes Barnaba (baritone), an Inquisition spy, with the promise of her own love to release Enzo from prison, and helps him escape from Venice with Laura. Barnaba arrives to take his reward, and Gioconda stabs herself.

Poulenc, Francis (1899–1963), French composer. Two sides of his musical personality, the elegantly satirical and the deeply religious, are well illustrated by his operas. *Les Mamelles de Tirésias* (The Breasts of Tiresias), a comic opera with text by Guillaume Apollinaire, first performed on 3 June 1947 at the Opéra-Comique, Paris, concerns Thérèse (soprano), who changes sex with her Husband (tenor or baritone). *Les Dialogues des Carmélites*, with text taken from a play by Georges Bernanos, first performed on 26 January 1957 at La Scala, Milan, is set in the Carmelite Convent of Compiègne and in Paris during the French Revolution. Blanche de la Force (soprano) enters the convent more out of fear than from conviction, and leaves it for the same reason, but finds the courage to die under the guillotine with the rest of the nuns. *La Voix humaine* (The Human Voice) is a one-act monologue with text by Jean Cocteau, in which a woman (soprano) holds a telephone conversation with her faithless lover before killing herself.

Rossini *Il barbiere di Siviglia*. Glyndebourne. 1981. Figaro (John Rawnsley), Rosina (Maria Ewing) (Guy Gravett)

R. Strauss *Elektra*. Welsh National Opera, 1978. Chrysothemis (Anne Evans), Elektra (Pauline Tinsley) (Welsh National Opera)

(*right*) R. Strauss *Die schweigsame Frau*. Glyndebourne, 1979. Isotta (Kate Flowers), Morosus (Marius Rintzler) (Guy Gravett)

(*below*) R. Strauss *Capriccio*. Glyndebourne, 1973. Countess Madeleine (Elisabeth Söderström) (Guy Gravett)

Tippett *King Priam*. Royal Opera Covent Garden, 1975. Hermes (Kenneth Bowen), Paris (Robert Tear) (Donald Southern)

Prokofiev, Sergei (1891–1953), Russian composer. The first three of Prokofiev's mature operas were premiered in the West in French translation. *The Gambler*, based on the novel by Dostoievsky, was first performed on 29 April 1929 at the Théâtre de la Monnaie, Brussels. *The Love of Three Oranges*, with text by the composer based on a comedy by Carlo Gozzi, was first performed on 30 December 1921 in Chicago. *The Fiery Angel* was first given in concert on 25 November 1954 in Paris, and first staged on 14 September 1955 in Venice. After Prokofiev's return to Russia, he composed four more operas, including *Betrothal in a Monastery*, with text by Mira Mendelson based on Sheridan's comedy *The Duenna*, first performed on 30 November 1946 at the Kirov Theatre, Leningrad; and *War and Peace*, with text by the composer and Mendelson adapted from Tolstoy's novel, first given in concert on 7 June 1945 in Moscow. It was not staged in anything like a full version until 1955, at the Maly Theatre, Leningrad.

Puccini, Giacomo (1858–1924), Italian composer. He scored his first great success with *Manon Lescaut* (1893), an adaptation of Prévost's novel, using mainly different episodes from Massenet's version of the story. *La Bohème* (1896), *Tosca* (1900) and *Madama Butterfly* (1904) confirmed Puccini's position as the most popular living operatic composer, though *Butterfly* was initially a total failure. *La fanciulla del West*, based on David Belasco's play, *The Girl of the Golden West*, and set in California, was first performed on 10 December 1910 at the Metropolitan, New York. *La rondine* (The Swallow), an operetta originally intended for Vienna, was first performed in 1917 at Monte Carlo. *Il trittico* (1918), a tryptich consisting of *Il tabarro* (The Cloak), *Suor Angelica* (Sister Angelica) and *Gianni Schicchi*, was premiered in New York. *Turandot* was left uncompleted at the composer's death.

La Bohème, opera in four acts with text by Giuseppe Giacosa and Luigi Illica based on *Scènes de la vie de Bohème* by Henri Murger. First performed on 1 February 1898 at Teatro Regio, Turin. Set in Paris about 1830.

ACT 1. The Bohemians, Rodolfo (tenor), a poet, Marcello (baritone), a painter, Schaunard (baritone), a musician, and Colline (bass), a philosopher, decide to celebrate Christmas Eve at the Café Momus. Rodolfo stays behind in their communal attic to finish an article, and makes the acquaintance of Mimi (soprano), a seamstress who comes in to obtain a light for her candle. He is greatly attracted to the girl, and she to him.

ACT 2. Rodolfo and Mimi join the other Bohemians outside the Café Momus. Musetta (soprano), an old flame of Marcello's, sits at the next table with her elderly admirer Alcindoro (bass), whom she gets rid of with the pretext of a painful shoe. There is a rapturous reunion between Marcello and Musetta, and the sextet go off, leaving Alcindoro to pay their bill as well as his own.

ACT 3. At the Barrière d'enfer, a gate into the city, Mimi comes to see Marcello, who is living at a nearby tavern with Musetta. Mimi complains of Rodolfo's jealousy, which makes their lives together impossible. She hides as Rodolfo comes out of the tavern, but her coughing betrays her presence. They decide regretfully that they will have to part, while Marcello and Musetta quarrel over the latter's flirtatiousness.

ACT 4. In the Bohemians' attic, Rodolfo and Marcello reminisce sadly about Mimi and Musetta, now living with other, richer admirers. Schaunard and Colline return, and the four indulge in horseplay until Musetta arrives with Mimi, who is dying of consumption. As the others go out to raise money to buy medicine for her, Mimi and Rodolfo recall the evening they first met. Musetta returns with a muff and Mimi falls asleep. A few minutes later Rodolfo finds that she is dead.

Tosca, opera in three acts, with text by Giacosa and Illica after the play by Victorien Sardou. First performed on 14 January 1900 at Teatro Costanzi, Rome. Set in Rome during June 1800.

ACT 1. Mario Cavaradossi (tenor) is painting a picture of Mary Magdalen in the church of Sant'Andrea della Valle, using as model a fair-haired woman who prays there frequently. She is the Marchesa Attavanti, sister to Cesare Angelotti (bass), a political prisoner who, having escaped from the Castel Sant'Angelo, takes refuge in the church and is helped by Cavaradossi. Angelotti hides in the Attavanti chapel when Floria Tosca (soprano), an opera singer, comes to see Cavaradossi, with whom she is living. Tosca, who is extremely jealous, recognizes the Magdalen as Marchesa Attavanti, but is pacified by her lover, and leaves. A cannon-shot announces the discovery of the prisoner's escape, and Angelotti and Cavaradossi hurry away to the latter's villa outside Rome. The Sacristan (bass) comes to announce a victory over Napoleon Bonaparte's troops. There is to be a *Te Deum* sung in celebration, and the choirboys tease and dance around him until the abrupt arrival of Baron Scarpia (baritone), the police chief, and his men, who have traced the escaped prisoner to the church. When Scarpia recognizes the painting of Marchesa Attavanti and finds her family chapel unlocked, he understands what has happened. Tosca returns, and Scarpia plays on her jealousy to make her believe that Cavaradossi and the Attavanti are having an affair. When she leaves he has her followed. The Cardinal's procession enters for the *Te Deum*.

ACT 2. In his apartment in the Palazzo Farnese, Scarpia is dining. His agent Spoletta (tenor) reports that he found no one at Cavaradossi's villa but the painter, whom he has arrested. Scarpia sends for Tosca, whose voice singing a cantata, also in celebration of the victory, can be heard through the window. Cavaradossi is brought in, but denies any knowledge of Angelotti. Having finished the cantata, Tosca comes in and Cavaradossi is taken to be questioned in an adjoining room. Scarpia describes to Tosca how her lover is being tortured. She could save him much pain if she revealed Angelotti's hiding-place. At first Tosca refuses to speak, but Cavaradossi's cries are too much for her and she tells Scarpia, 'The well, in the garden.' Cavaradossi is carried in. Tosca assures him that she did not speak, but when Scarpia gives Spoletta precise instructions on where to find Angelotti, Cavaradossi knows that Tosca betrayed him. News is brought that the defeat of Napoleon has been turned to victory for the Bonapartist troops at Marengo. Exultantly, Cavaradossi declares his joy and is taken off for execution. Tosca asks Scarpia his price for her lover's freedom, and the answer is herself. She hesitates, but the sound of drums from the military escort that will accompany Cavaradossi to the scaffold makes her agree to the bargain. Spoletta is given instructions: Cavaradossi is to be shot, not hung, in a faked execution. Tosca demands a safe-conduct from Scarpia, then, rather than submit to his embraces, she stabs him with a fruit knife from the dining table. Pausing only to put candles on either side of Scarpia's body, and a crucifix on his breast, she hurries out.

ACT 3. On the platform of Castel Sant'Angelo, Cavaradossi awaits execution at dawn. He bribes the jailer to let him write a letter to Tosca, but she herself comes to tell him of Scarpia's death and of the fake execution. The firing party arrives, a volley is fired, and Cavaradossi falls to the ground. When the soldiers have gone, Tosca runs to her lover, calling him to get up, but Cavaradossi is dead. The execution was not faked but real. Tosca climbs on to the balustrade and leaps to her death in the River Tiber below.

Madama Butterfly, opera in three acts (originally two) with text by Giacosa and Illica after the play by David Belasco. First performed on 17 February 1904 at La Scala, Milan. Set in contemporary Nagasaki, Japan.

ACT 1. In a house overlooking the harbour, Lieutenant Pinkerton (tenor) of the US Navy is about to marry Cio-Cio-San, or Butterfly (soprano), in a ceremony that, as he tells the American consul, Sharpless (baritone), he does not consider binding. Butterfly, her relations and friends arrive for the wedding. The Bonze (bass), Butterfly's uncle, curses her for renouncing her faith, and the relations and friends hurriedly leave. Pinkerton comforts Butterfly, and they express their love for each other.

ACT 2. Three years have passed. Butterfly and her servant Suzuki (mezzo-soprano) have spent nearly all the money that Pinkerton left them when his ship sailed from Nagasaki. Goro (tenor), the marriage-broker, wants Butterfly to marry the rich Prince Yamadori (baritone), but she considers herself still Madam Pinkerton. The Consul comes to read her a letter from Pinkerton, who is now married to an American wife and on his way back to Japan. Butterfly will not listen to his warning that Pinkerton might not return to her, and shows the Consul her child, born after his father's departure. A ship is sighted entering the harbour, and Butterfly and Suzuki, identifying the *Abraham Lincoln*, decorate the house with flowers. Then, with her child, Butterfly waits at the window for Pinkerton.

ACT 3. After a night-long vigil, Butterfly is resting when Pinkerton, accompanied by his wife Kate (mezzo-soprano) and the Consul, eventually arrives. He has come to ask Butterfly to give up her child, and Suzuki is deputed to tell Cio-Cio-San of the demand. Butterfly agrees, stipulating only that Pinkerton should himself fetch the boy. Then, with the dagger that her father had received from the Emperor with orders to commit hari-kiri, she kills herself.

Turandot, opera in three acts, completed by Alfano, with text by G. Adami and R. Simoni, after a play by Carlo Gozzi. First performed on 25 April 1926 at La Scala, Milan. Set in Peking in legendary times.

ACT 1. Turandot (soprano), beautiful daughter of Emperor Altoum (tenor), asks her suitors three riddles. If they cannot answer correctly they are executed, and so far no suitor has survived. Calaf (tenor), son of Timur (bass), the blind and exiled King of Tartary, meets his father and the slave-girl Liù (soprano), who looks after him, in the courtyard of the palace, where crowds wait for the execution of Turandot's latest victim. The Princess appears to give the death signal, and Calaf is so overcome by her beauty that, despite the pleas of his father and of Liù, he strikes the gong, signifying that he wishes to undergo the trial himself.

ACT 2. Ping (baritone), Pang and Pong (tenors), three of Altoum's ministers, lament the change that has come over China since the days of their youth. The crowd gathers for the unknown Prince's trial. Turandot relates the story of her ancestress, ravished by a foreign conqueror centuries earlier, and the reason for Turandot's own revenge on her suitors. Three riddles are asked and Calaf answers them all correctly. Turandot pleads with her father not to give her to the unknown Prince. Altoum insists that she has been fairly won, but Calaf offers to die if Turandot can find out his name before dawn.

ACT 3. Calaf waits for dawn, while Turandot's guards search for clues to his identity. Timur and Liù, who were seen in the unknown Prince's company, are brought in and Liù, who claims that she alone knows the secret, is tortured but refuses to betray the man she loves. Fearing that her strength to resist may run out, she kills herself. Calaf, left alone with Turandot, gradually thaws the ice in her heart. As the sun comes up he tells her his name—Calaf. In triumph Turandot tells the Emperor that she knows the stranger's name—it is Love.

Purcell, Henry (1659–95), English composer. Though he composed only one opera, *Dido and Aeneas*, several of his masques have been adapted and revived in the present century. These include *The Fairy Queen* (1692), based on Shakespeare's *A Midsummer Night's Dream*; *King Arthur*, or *The British Worthy* (1691), with text by Dryden; *The Tempest*, or *The Enchanted Isle* (1695), another adaptation of Shakespeare; and *The Indian Queen* (1695).

Dido and Aeneas, opera in three acts with text by Nahum Tate after Virgil's *Aeneid*, was first performed in 1689 or 1690 at Josias Priest's School for Young Gentlewomen, and publicly staged in 1700.

ACT 1. Dido, Queen of Carthage (soprano), is tormented by an emotion that her Lady, Belinda (soprano), correctly guesses to be love for the Trojan hero Aeneas (baritone). Aeneas arrives to pay court to Dido.

The Sorceress (mezzo-soprano) and Witches plan the downfall of Dido and the destruction of Carthage.

ACT 2. Dido, Aeneas and the Court are picnicking during a hunt when it begins to rain. As they return to the city, Aeneas is stopped by one of the Sorceress's minions disguised as Mercury, who reminds him of his mission to rebuild Troy in Latium.

ACT 3. By the harbour, sailors dance and sing. The Sorceress and Witches celebrate the success of their plan. Dido and Belinda come to find Aeneas, who admits he is forced to leave Carthage. When the Trojan fleet has sailed, Dido prepares for her death.

Rameau, Jean-Philippe (1683–1764), French composer. His many successful operas and opera-ballets include *Hippolyte et Aricie* (1733), *Les Indes galantes* (1735), *Castor et Pollux* (1737), *Dardanus* (1739), *Naïs* and *Zoroastre* (1749), all first performed at the Paris Opéra.

Ravel, Maurice (1875–1937), French composer. His first opera, *L'Heure espagnole* (The Spanish Hour), with text by Franc-Nohain, produced in 1911 at the Opéra-Comique, Paris, is a comedy. Concepcion (soprano), wife to Torquemada (tenor), clockmaker of Toledo, prefers the muleteer Ramiro (baritone) to either of her admirers, the poet Gonzalve (tenor) and the banker Don Inigo Gomez (bass). Ravel's second opera, *L'Enfant et les sortilèges* (The Child and the Spells), with text by Colette, was first performed in 1925 at Monte Carlo. A Child (mezzo-soprano) loses his temper and is admonished first by the furniture (chairs, clock, teapot, cup, etc) and then by the garden birds and animals (nightingale, owl, squirrel, bat and dragonfly).

Rimsky-Korsakov, Nikolay (1844–1908), Russian composer. His 15 operas were mainly based on Russian history or derived from Russian legends and fairy tales. *The Maid of Pskov* (1873) and *The Tsar's Bride* (1899) fall into the first category. *A May Night* (1880), *The Snow Maiden* (1882), *Sadko* (1898), *The Story of Tsar Saltan* (1900) and *The Legend of the Invisible City of Kitezh* (1907) fall into the second. *The Golden Cockerel*, Rimsky-Korsakov's last and best-known opera, with text based on a poem by Pushkin, also legendary in subject, was posthumously produced on 7 October 1909 in Moscow.

Rossini, Gioacchino (1792–1868), Italian composer. Several of his early operas were popular in Italy, among them *La pietra del paragone* (The Touchstone), his first work premiered at La Scala, Milan (1812). But Rossini's enormous popularity throughout Europe really began with his tenth opera, *Tancredi*, first performed in 1813 at Teatro la Fenice, Venice. During the next decade more than 20 operas flowed from his facile pen. Comic successes included *L'italiana in Algerì* (1813), *Il turco in Italia* (1814), *Il barbiere di Siviglia* (1816), *La cenerentola* (1817) and the semi-serious *La gazza ladra* (The Thieving Magpie), produced in 1817 at La Scala. His serious operas of the period include *Elisabetta, regina d'Inghilterra* (1815); *Otello* (1816), a much-altered version of Shakespeare's play; *Mosè in Egitto* (1818); *La donna del lago* (1819), based on Walter Scott's poem *The Lady of the Lake*; and *Maometto II* (1820), all first produced at Naples. *Semiramide* (1823), first performed at La Fenice, Venice, was Rossini's last opera to be composed for a theatre in Italy.

Rossini's last four operas were settings of French texts. *Le Siège de Corinthe* (1826) and *Moïse et Pharaon* (1827) were reworkings of, respectively, *Maometto II* and *Mosè in Egitto*. Like *Le Comte Ory* (1828) and *Guillaume Tell* (1829), they were first performed at the Paris Opéra.

Il barbiere di Siviglia (The Barber of Seville), opera in two acts with text by Cesare Sterbini after the comedy by Beaumarchais. First performed on 20 February 1816 at Teatro Argentina, Rome.

ACT 1. Count Almaviva (tenor), disguised as the student Lindoro, serenades Rosina (mezzo-soprano), ward of Doctor Bartolo (bass), who plans to marry her himself. Aided by the barber Figaro (baritone), Almaviva gains admittance to Bartolo's house disguised as a drunken soldier. During the ensuing uproar he makes plain his tender feelings for Rosina.

ACT 2. Almaviva, disguised this time as Don Alonso, a pupil of Don Basilio (bass), Rosina's singing teacher, re-enters Bartolo's house. While Figaro is shaving the Doctor, Almaviva makes arrangements to elope with Rosina that evening. Almaviva and Figaro get into the house by means of a ladder to the balcony. The Count and Rosina are married by the notary that Bartolo has summoned for his own proposed marriage to his ward.

La cenerentola (Cinderella), opera in two acts with text by Jacopo Ferretti after the fairy tale by Perrault. First performed on 25 January 1817 at Teatro Valle, Rome.

Clorinda (soprano) and Thisbe (mezzo-soprano), daughters of Don Magnifico (bass), are invited to the ball given by Don Ramiro, Prince of Salerno. Angelina (contralto), Magnifico's stepdaughter (known as Cinderella), is left at home until Alidoro (bass), philosopher and friend to the Prince, comes to escort her to the palace. At the ball, Clorinda and Thisbe quarrel over the 'Prince', who is in reality Dandini (baritone), his valet. Ramiro (tenor), disguised as Dandini, falls in love with the unknown lady, looking suspiciously like Cinderella, who arrives with Alidoro.

Returning home, Clorinda and Thisbe find Cinderella in the kitchen. During a storm the Prince's carriage breaks down outside Don Magnifico's house. Don Ramiro, seeking shelter, recognizes Cinderella and asks her to be his wife. In her happiness, Angelina forgives her stepfather and sisters for their cruelty.

Le Comte Ory, opera in two acts with text by Eugène Scribe and Delestre-Poirson, first performed on 20 August 1828 at the Paris Opéra. Set in Touraine during the Crusades.

ACT 1. Count Ory (tenor) disguises himself as a hermit in order to get inside the castle of Fourmoutiers where the beautiful Countess Adèle (soprano) has immured herself during her brother's absence at the Crusades. His plan is foiled by his page Isolier (mezzo-soprano), who also loves Adèle.

ACT 2. Ory, his friend Raimbaud (baritone), his tutor (bass) and his cavaliers infiltrate the castle dressed as pilgrim sisters, but again it is Isolier who thwarts the evil designs of the 'mother-superior'. Ory and his friends beat an ignominious retreat just as the knights return from the Crusades.

Guillaume Tell, opera in four acts with text by E. de Jouy and H. L. F. Bis, based on Schiller's play. First performed on 3 August 1829 at the Paris Opéra. Set in thirteenth-century Switzerland.

William Tell (baritone), Arnold (tenor) and their supporters swear to rid their country of the Austrian tyrant Gessler (bass), who was responsible for the death of Arnold's father Melcthal (bass). Tell refuses to salute Gessler's hat set on a pole in the market-place, and Gessler orders him to shoot at an apple placed on the head of his son, Jemmy (soprano). Tell succeeds and Gessler orders his arrest, but the Swiss rise against their Austrian oppressors and Gessler is killed. Arnold is reunited with Mathilde (soprano), Gessler's sister, whom he loves.

Saint-Saëns, Camille (1835–1921), French composer. He wrote a dozen operas, including *La Princesse jaune* (1872), *Henry VIII* (1883), *Ascanio* (1890), *Phryné* (1893) and *Hélène* (1904), but only *Samson et Dalila* is still performed today. Based on the biblical story in the Book of Judges, *Samson et Dalila* was first performed on 2 December 1877, in German translation, at Weimar. The first French performance was not until 3 March 1890 at Rouen, but the work's tremendous popularity dates from its entry into the Paris Opéra repertory in 1892. Samson (tenor), the Israelite hero, leads his people in a successful uprising against the Philistines. Dalila (mezzo-soprano) promises the High Priest of Dagon (baritone) that she will discover the secret of Samson's strength. Samson succumbs to Dalila's seductive charms and, shorn of his hair, is captured by the Philistines. Blinded and a slave, Samson is jeered at by the Philistines as they celebrate their victory over the Israelites. With a last exertion of his old strength, Samson pulls down the pillars of the Temple of Dagon.

Schoenberg, Arnold (1874–1951), Austrian composer. His first opera, *Erwartung* (Expectation), composed in 1909, was first performed on 6 June 1924 at Prague. The single character, a woman (soprano), searches for her lover in a dark wood and eventually discovers his dead body. *Von Heute auf Morgen* (From Day to Day), composed in 1921 and produced on 1 February 1930 at Frankfurt, was the first wholly dodecaphonic opera. After completing the first two acts of *Moses und Aron* in 1932, Schoenberg never finished the third. With text by the composer, *Moses und Aron* was first staged on 6 June 1957 at Zurich. Moses (bass-baritone/speaker), unable to communicate his revelation of the word of God, allows his brother Aaron (tenor) to explain it to the people by means of miracles. During Moses' absence on Sinai, the people worship the idol of the Golden Calf. Moses despairs of his ability to communicate his message without the distortion of a mouthpiece such as Aaron.

Shostakovich, Dmitry (1906–75), Russian composer. His early satirical opera, *The Nose*, based on a story by Gogol, was first performed on 12 January 1930 at the Maly Theatre, Leningrad. *Katerina Ismailova*, originally entitled *The Lady Macbeth of the Mtsensk Districts,* was first performed on 22 January 1934, also at the Maly

Theatre, Leningrad. Withdrawn after a violent onslaught against the composer in *Pravda*, the opera was revived, in a revised version, in 1963. Katerina (soprano) and her lover Sergei (tenor) are discovered by her father-in-law Boris (bass). Boris has Sergei flogged and sends for his son Zinovy (tenor), who is away on business. Katerina poisons the mushrooms Boris eats for supper, releases Sergei and together with him kills Zinovy on his arrival home. The body, hidden in the cellar, is discovered during the celebrations for Katerina's wedding to Sergei. Both are convicted of murder and sent to Siberia, where Katerina, deserted by Sergei for Sonyetka (contralto), drowns her rival and herself in the river.

Smetana, Bedřich (1824–84), Czech composer. He wrote three patriotic operas on Czech nationalist themes: *The Brandenburgers in Bohemia* (1866), *Dalibor* (1868) and *Libuše* (1881), as well as three comic operas: *The Two Widows* (1874), *The Kiss* (1876) and *The Secret* (1878). It is *The Bartered Bride*, combining nationalist and comic elements, that has become his best-loved opera, both inside and outside Czechoslovakia.

The Bartered Bride, opera in three acts (originally two) with text by K. Sabina, first performed on 30 May 1866 at the Provisional Theatre, Prague. Set in a Bohemian village.

Mařenka (soprano) is in love with Jeník (tenor) though her parents, Krušina (baritone) and Ludmila (mezzo-soprano), want her to accept a husband proposed by Kečal (bass), the marriage-broker. The candidate is Vašek (tenor), son of Micha (bass) and his wife Hata (mezzo-soprano). To Mařenka's despair, Jeník sells his claim to her to Kečal for 300 gulden, stipulating only that her husband must be the son of Tobias Micha. When Mařenka signs the contract, it is to discover that her bridegroom is Jenik himself—he is Micha's long-lost elder son.

Spontini, Gasparo (1774–1851), Italian composer. Between 1796 and 1802 he wrote more than a dozen operas for various Italian theatres. He then went to Paris, where he had three works performed at the Opéra-Comique, including *Milton* (1804). *La Vestale* (1807), with text by Étienne de Jouy, *Fernand Cortez* (1809) and *Olympie* (1819), all produced at the Opéra, were prototypes of French grand opera. *Agnes von Hohenstauffen* (1829), with German text by E. Raupach, was performed at the Court Opera, Berlin.

Strauss, Johann II (1825–99), Austrian composer. The most successful of his operettas, *Die Fledermaus* (The Bat), was first performed on 5 April 1874 at the Theater an der Wien, Vienna, and has maintained its position as the world's favourite Viennese operetta for over a century. *Der Zigeunerbaron,* or the Gypsy Baron (1885), is still frequently performed but *Ritter Pasman* (1893), the work with which Strauss first stormed the portals of the Vienna Court Opera, has been less lucky.

Strauss, Richard (1864–1949), German composer. His first opera, *Guntram* (1894), was politely received at Weimar, but a disastrous single performance in his home-town of Munich resulted in *Feuersnot* (Fire Famine), first performed in 1901 at Dresden, in which the young magician (Strauss himself), aided by the old magician (Richard Wagner), scores a symbolic victory over the townspeople of Munich. With the production of *Salome* (1905), banned from many theatres for its shocking treatment of a biblical subject, Strauss became the most famous living German composer. *Elektra* (1909) introduced him to the Austrian poet and playwright, Hugo von Hofmannsthal, who provided Strauss with texts for *Der Rosenkavalier* (1911), *Ariadne auf Naxos* (1912), *Die Frau ohne Schatten* (1919), *Die Ägyptisches Helena* (1928) and *Arabella* (1933). Strauss wrote the text himself for *Intermezzo*, produced in 1924 at Dresden, in which he and his wife Pauline are thinly disguised as Robert and Christine Storch, and which is based on an incident that had happened some 20 years before. After Hofmannsthal's death Strauss found a new collaborator in Stefan Zweig, who provided the text for *Die schweigsame Frau* (1935), based on Ben Jonson's play *Epicoene*, or *The Silent Woman*. But Zweig was forced to leave Germany by the rising tide of Nazism. The texts of Strauss's next three operas, *Friedenstag* (Day of Peace) and *Daphne* (1938), and *Die Liebe der Danae* (The Love of Danae), completed in 1940 but not publicly performed until 1952 at Salzburg, were by Josef Gregor. Strauss's lifelong devotion to the marriage between words and music was summed up in his last opera *Capriccio*.

Salome, opera in one act, with text from Oscar Wilde's tragedy, translated by H. Lachmann. First performed on 9 December 1905 at the Hofoper, Dresden. Set in Tiberias, about AD 30.

Salome (soprano), daughter of Herodias (mezzo-soprano), the wife of Herod (tenor), is fascinated by the prophet Jokanaan, or John the Baptist (baritone). Because Jokanaan rejects her advances, Salome demands his head on a silver platter as reward for the dance she performs for Herod but, when she kisses the lips of the severed head, she finds them strangely bitter. Herod orders the guards to kill her.

Elektra, opera in one act with text taken from Hofmannsthal's play, itself derived from Sophocles' tragedy. First performed on 25 January 1909 at the Hofoper, Dresden. Set in Mycenae.

Elektra (soprano), daughter of Agamemnon, who

was murdered by his wife Klytemnestra (mezzo-soprano) and her lover Aegisth (tenor), is treated as a slave in her mother's palace. News is brought that Orest (baritone), Agamemnon's son, has been killed. But the messenger is Orest himself, come to avenge his father, though brother and sister do not at first recognize each other. After Orest has killed Klytemnestra and Aegisth, Elektra dances in wild exultation and collapses dead.

Der Rosenkavalier (The Knight of the Rose), opera in three acts with text by Hofmannsthal, first performed on 26 January 1911 at the Hofoper, Dresden. Set in Vienna during the reign of the Empress Maria Theresa.

ACT 1. The Marschallin (soprano), wife of the Field Marshall, is having an affair with a much younger man, Oktavian (soprano), during her husband's absence. Surprised in the Marschallin's bedroom by the early morning visit of Baron Ochs (bass), Oktavian dresses as Mariandel, the Marschallin's maid. Ochs has come to ask the Marschallin to recommend a young nobleman to act as rose-bearer to his prospective bride, Sophie von Faninal. The Marschallin suggests Count Oktavian, and Ochs is struck by the likeness of his portrait to Mariandel, whom he greatly fancies. After the levée, in which the Marschallin receives an Italian singer (tenor), her Notary, a Dressmaker and various other petitioners, Oktavian returns in his own clothes to find her in a pensive mood; she knows the time to give him up to someone younger will soon arrive.

ACT 2. Oktavian comes to Faninal's house to present Sophie (soprano) with the Silver Rose on behalf of Ochs. The two young people are mutually attracted, and Sophie is shocked by the boorish behaviour of her prospective bridegroom when he arrives with Faninal (baritone). While Ochs and Faninal are closeted with the Notary, Oktavian and Sophie are discovered in each other's arms by two Italian intriguers, Valzacchi (tenor) and Annina (mezzo-soprano). In the ensuing fracas, Oktavian draws his sword and slightly wounds the Baron in the arm. Ochs makes a tremendous fuss about the scratch, but his good humour is restored when Annina brings him a letter from Mariandel, making an assignation.

ACT 3. At the inn where the assignation with the Baron is about to take place, Oktavian, again dressed as Mariandel, completes his plans for Ochs's discomfiture. The Baron arrives and sits down to supper with Mariandel, but her likeness to Oktavian unnerves him. He is further upset when a veiled woman—Annina—rushes in claiming to be his deserted wife. Ochs sends for the police; Faninal and Sophie arrive, summoned by Valzacchi, and finally the Marschallin herself makes an entrance. She pacifies the Police Commissioner (bass) and tells Ochs that his betrothal to Sophie is off. When the Baron has fled, followed by the innkeeper and the other creditors, she goes to intercede with Faninal on behalf of Oktavian and Sophie. Left alone, the young lovers express their happiness.

Ariadne auf Naxos, opera in one act with text by Hofmannsthal, originally designed to follow his translated version of Molière's comedy *Le Bourgeois gentilhomme*. First performed on 25 October 1912 at Stuttgart; second version, with Prologue by Strauss and Hofmannsthal, first performed on 4 October 1916 at the Hofoper, Vienna.

The Prologue is set in the house of the richest man in Vienna, who has commissioned an opera, *Ariadne on Naxos*, from the Composer (soprano) and a Harlequinade to follow it. The Majordomo (speaking role) announces that the two entertainments will have to be performed together, so that the fireworks display can start at nine o'clock. The Composer's despair is momentarily lightened by the attractions of Zerbinetta (soprano), leader of the Harlequinade, but for him there can be no compromise: music is a sacred art.

The opera is set on the island of Naxos, where Ariadne (soprano), abandoned by Theseus, waits for death. All attempts by Zerbinetta and her four companions (two tenors, baritone and bass) to cheer her up are useless. A ship approaches and the young god Bacchus (tenor) comes ashore. Ariadne at first takes him for Mercury, the harbinger of death, but then accepts him as a new lover, just as Zerbinetta had advised.

Die Frau ohne Schatten (The Woman Without a Shadow), opera in three acts with text by Hofmannsthal, first performed on 10 October 1919 at the Staatsoper, Vienna.

The Emperor (tenor) has married the daughter of Keikobad, the Spirit King. During her husband's absence on a hunting expedition, the Empress (soprano), with her Nurse (mezzo-soprano), descends to Earth to find a shadow, the symbol of fertility. If she does not find one within three days, the Emperor will be turned to stone. The Dyer's Wife (soprano), a dissatisfied young woman who longs for love and riches without the trouble of childbearing, is selected by the Nurse as someone likely to sell her shadow. But the simple goodness of Barak (baritone), the Dyer, so impresses the Empress that she refuses to drink the Water of Life, even to save her husband. She is granted a shadow and the two couples, happily reunited, hear the voices of their unborn children.

Arabella, opera in three acts with text by Hofmannsthal, first performed on 1 July 1933 at the Staatsoper, Dresden. Set in Vienna about 1860.

ACT 1. Count Waldner (bass) and his wife Adelaide (mezzo-soprano) have come to Vienna to find a rich husband for their elder daughter Arabella (soprano), meanwhile dressing their younger daughter Zdenka (soprano) as a boy, to save expense. Arabella likes none of her suitors enough to marry him, though a stranger she sees in the street catches her fancy. Waldner receives a visit from Mandryka (baritone), nephew of the Count's old regimental comrade, now dead, to whom he had sent a photograph of his daughter. Mandryka, a rich Croatian landowner, applies formally for Arabella's hand.

ACT 2. At the Cabbies' Ball that evening, Mandryka is introduced to Arabella. She accepts him, recognizing the stranger she noticed earlier, and says goodbye to her suitors. Matteo (tenor), a penniless officer to whom Zdenka (who is in love with him herself) has been writing letters in her sister's name, is in despair until Arabella's 'brother' gives him a key—the key to Arabella's bedroom. Mandryka overhears the episode and, receiving a note from Arabella to say that she has returned to the hotel, believes the worst.

ACT 3. Back at the hotel, Matteo, emerging from what he takes to be her bedroom, is amazed to see Arabella a few minutes later in the lobby. Mandryka, arriving with the Waldners from the ball, accuses Arabella of unfaithfulness. The situation is resolved only when Zdenka, in her nightdress, runs downstairs. Waldner accepts Matteo as Zdenka's suitor and everyone goes off to bed. Arabella asks for a glass of water to be brought to her room, then descends the stairs to offer it to Mandryka, as in the Croatian betrothal ceremony he had described earlier in the evening.

Capriccio, opera in one act, with text by Clemens Krauss, suggested by *Prima la musica e poi le parole* (First the Music and Then the Words), an opera by Salieri (1786). First performed on 28 October 1942 at Munich. Set in a château near Paris about 1775.

The Countess Madeleine, a young widow (soprano), has two admirers, the musician Flamand (tenor) and the poet Olivier (baritone), and cannot decide which she prefers. Various entertainments are rehearsed in honour of her birthday. The Count (baritone), her brother, is taking part in a play with the celebrated actress Clairon (mezzo-soprano), while La Roche (bass), a theatre director, presents a young dancer and two Italian singers (soprano and tenor). During a general discussion it is suggested that Olivier and Flamand should write an opera, not on the usual mythological subject but on the day's events. Left alone, the Countess still cannot decide how the opera should end.

Stravinsky, Igor (1882–1971), Russian, later French, then American, composer. His first opera, *The Nightingale*, based on a fairy tale by Hans Andersen, was produced in 1914 at the Paris Opéra. Two short works, *Renard*, based on Russian folk tales, and *Mavra*, drawn from a poem by Pushkin, were first performed together in 1922, also at the Paris Opéra.

Oedipus Rex, with text by Jean Cocteau after the tragedy by Sophocles, translated into Latin, was sung as an oratorio on 30 May 1927 in Paris and first staged in the following year at Vienna. Oedipus (tenor), seeking to unmask the murderer of Laius, his predecessor as King of Thebes, discovers that he himself is the murderer and that, as the son of Laius and Queen Jocasta (mezzo-soprano), now his wife, he has killed his father and married his mother. The Messenger (bass-baritone) describes how Jocasta kills herself and Oedipus blinds himself with her golden pin.

Stravinsky's last full-length opera, *The Rake's Progress*, in three acts, with English text by W. H. Auden and Chester Kallman based on the series of engravings by Hogarth, was first performed on 11 September 1951 at Teatro la Fenice, Venice. The opera is set in eighteenth-century England.

Tom Rakewell (tenor) learns from Nick Shadow (baritone) that he has inherited money and, deserting his betrothed Anne Trulove (soprano), sets up as a gentleman of fashion, with Nick as his servant, in London. Dissipation and marriage to Baba the Turk (mezzo-soprano), a Bearded Lady, lead him to bankruptcy and the auction of his property. Nick claims his wages—Tom's soul—but agrees to stake them on a game of cards. Tom wins, saving his soul but losing his reason. In Bedlam, Anne comes to visit Tom for the last time. He thinks he is Adonis and takes her for Venus.

Tchaikovsky, Pytor Ilych (1840–93), Russian composer. His first opera, *The Voyevoda* (1869), was produced at the Bolshoi Theatre, Moscow. *The Oprichnik* (1874), *Vakula the Smith* (1876) and *The Maid of Orleans* (1881), with text by the composer based on Schiller's play, were first performed in St Petersburg at the Maryinsky Theatre. *Mazeppa* (1884), derived from a poem by Pushkin, and *Cherevichki* (1887), a revised version of *Vakula the Smith*, were premiered in Moscow. *The Sorceress* (1887) and *Yolanta* (1892) were premiered in St Petersburg. None of these operas was particularly successful. Tchaikovsky's operatic masterpiece is undoubtedly *Eugene Onegin*, with *The Queen of Spades* as second favourite.

Eugene Onegin, opera in three acts with text by the composer and K. S. Shilovsky based on Pushkin's verse novel. First performed on 29 March 1879 at the Maly Theatre, Moscow. Set in Russia in the late eighteenth century.

ACT 1. Tatiana (soprano), daughter of Madame Larina (mezzo-soprano), falls in love with Eugene Onegin (baritone) when he accompanies his friend Lensky (tenor), who is engaged to Tatiana's sister Olga (contralto), on a visit to the Larina country estate.

Tatiana writes Onegin a letter expressing her love, which he, correctly but coldly, rejects.

ACT 2. At a dance at the Larinas', Onegin provokes his friend by monopolizing Olga. Lensky challenges him to a duel and is killed.

ACT 3. Some years later, at a ball in St Petersburg, Onegin meets Tatiana, now married to Prince Gremin (bass), and falls passionately in love with her. She admits that she still loves him, but as Gremin's wife she is no longer free.

The Queen of Spades, opera in three acts with text by the composer and his brother, Modest Tchaikovsky, based on a story by Pushkin. First performed on 19 December 1890 at the Maryinsky Theatre, St Petersburg. Set in St Petersburg in the late eighteenth century.

ACT 1. Herman (tenor), a penniless young officer, has fallen in love with Lisa (soprano), granddaughter of the Countess (mezzo-soprano), though she is engaged to marry Prince Yeletsky (baritone). Count Tomsky (baritone) relates a story about the Countess: a great beauty and an inveterate gambler in her youth, she bought with her favours the secret of the three cards from the Count of Saint-Germain. Twice she has revealed the secret; the third time she will die.

Herman gains entrance to Lisa's room by means of the balcony and declares his love, which she returns.

ACT 2. At a masked ball, Herman meets Lisa, who gives him a key to her room, which can be reached through her grandmother's apartments.

In the Countess's bedroom, Herman hides as he hears the old woman returning from the ball. Once in her nightgown, the Countess dismisses her maids and sits in a chair, remembering other parties long ago when she was young. Herman, intent on obtaining the secret of the three cards, appears before her. He draws a pistol and she dies of fright.

ACT 3. While the funeral of the Countess takes place, Herman, in his quarters at the barracks, is visited by her ghost. It gives him the secret of the three cards: Three, Seven, Ace.

At midnight, by the canal, Lisa meets Herman. He is obsessed by the thought of winning a fortune and rushes off to the gambling-house. In despair, Lisa throws herself in the canal.

Herman arrives at the gambling-house. He wins twice, on the Three and the Seven. Then Yeletsky accepts his challenge for the third round. Herman calls an Ace, but his card is the Queen of Spades. As he sees the Countess's ghost once more, Herman stabs himself.

Thomas, Ambroise (1811–96), French composer. He wrote many works for the Opéra-Comique, of which *Mignon*, with text by Barbier and Carré based on Goethe's novel, *Wilhelm Meister*, was much the most successful. It received nearly 2,000 performances in the century since its premiere on 17 November 1866. Of his works written for the Paris Opéra, *Hamlet* (1868), an adaptation by Barbier and Carré of Shakespeare's tragedy, is the best-known.

Tippett, (Sir) Michael (born 1905), English composer. His four operas, for which he wrote the texts himself, are *The Midsummer Marriage* (1955), *The Knot Garden* (1970) and *The Ice Break* (1977), all first performed at Covent Garden; and *King Priam* (1962), based on Homer's *Iliad*, first produced at Coventry.

Vaughan Williams, Ralph (1872–1958), English composer. His operas include *Hugh the Drover* (1924);

Sir John in Love (1929), based on Shakespeare's *The Merry Wives of Windsor*; *The Poisoned Kiss* (1936); *Riders to the Sea* (1937), a setting of the play by J. M. Synge; and *The Pilgrim's Progress* (1951), adapted from Bunyan, which was first produced at Covent Garden.

Verdi, Giuseppe (1813–1901), Italian composer. Between *Oberto, Conte di San Bonifacio*, first produced at La Scala, Milan in 1839, and *Falstaff*, premiered at the same theatre in 1893, Verdi composed two dozen operas that can be roughly divided into three periods. After the single, disastrous performance of *Un giorno di regno* (King For a Day) at La Scala in 1840, Verdi wrote no other comic operas until *Falstaff*, more than half a century later. For a decade, operas poured from his pen: *Nabucco* (1842); *I Lombardi alla prima crociata*, or The Lombards at the First Crusade (1843); *Ernani* and *I due Foscari* (1844); *Giovanna d'arco* (Joan of Arc), based on Schiller's play *The Maid of Orleans*, and *Alzira* (1845), based on the tragedy by Voltaire; *Attila* (1846); *Macbeth* and *I masnadieri*, or The Bandits (1847), a version of Schiller's play, first performed at Her Majesty's Theatre, London; *Il corsaro* (1848), after Byron's poem *The Corsair*; *La battaglia di Legnano* and *Luisa Miller* (1849).

Luisa Miller marks the beginning of Verdi's great middle period. *Stiffelio* (1850), later revised as *Aroldo* (1857), with the setting of early nineteenth-century Germany changed to twelfth-century Britain, was followed by *Rigoletto* (1851), *Il trovatore* and *La traviata* (1853), destined to become three of the most popular operas ever written. *Les Vêpres siciliennes* (The Sicilian Vespers), with text by E. Scribe and C. Duveyrier, Verdi's first setting of an original French text (*Jérusalem*, produced in 1847 at the Paris Opéra, is a revised version of *I Lombardi*), was performed on 13 June 1855 at the Opéra. *Simon Boccanegra* (1857), *Un ballo in maschera*

(1859) and *La forza del destino* (1862) bring the second period to an end. *Don Carlos* (1867), Verdi's second French opera, inaugurates the final period, which also includes *Aida* (1871), *Otello* (1887) and *Falstaff* (1893).

Nabucco, opera in four acts with libretto by T. Solera, first performed on 9 March 1842 at La Scala, Milan. Set in Jerusalem and Babylon in 586 BC.

ACT 1. Nabucco, or Nebuchadnezzar, King of Babylon (baritone), has defeated the Hebrews. Abigaille (soprano), supposedly Nabucco's daughter but in reality a slave, conquers the Temple, which is burnt to the ground on Nabucco's orders.

ACT 2. In Babylon, Abigaille discovers the secret of her lowly birth. She plans to take the crown from Fenena (soprano), Nabucco's daughter, who is acting as regent in her father's absence, but Nabucco returns, regains the crown and announces that he is the only god. A thunderbolt strikes him mad and Abigaille seizes power.

ACT 3. Abigaille forces Nabucco to sign the death sentence on the Hebrew captives, including Fenena. Fenena loves Ismaele (tenor), nephew of the King of Jerusalem, and has embraced the Jewish faith. On the banks of the Euphrates the Hebrews lament the loss of their homeland. Zaccaria (bass), a prophet, rouses them from their despair.

ACT 4. Nabucco prays to the Hebrew God and, regaining his sanity, goes to save Fenena from execution. The idol of Baal is miraculously shattered and the Jews are released. Abigaille, who has taken poison, dies repentant.

Ernani, opera in four acts with text by F. M. Piave based on Victor Hugo's play *Hernani*. First performed on 9 March 1844 at Teatro la Fenice, Venice. Set in Spain in 1519.

Ernani (tenor), the bandit, who is really the outlawed

Don John of Aragon, loves Elvira (soprano). She is about to be married to her guardian, the elderly Don Ruy Gomez de Silva (bass), and has a third suitor in Don Carlo (baritone), King Charles V of Spain. The sacred laws of hospitality force Silva to protect Ernani from the King's soldiers and, when Carlo abducts Elvira, the rivals temporarily become allies, planning to rescue Elvira and kill the King. By the tomb of Charlemagne in the cathedral of Aix-la-Chapelle, Carlo hears that he has been elected Holy Roman Emperor and confounds the conspirators. Magnanimously he pardons Ernani and gives Elvira to him in marriage. But as soon as the ceremony has taken place, Ernani hears the sound of a horn, the signal for him to kill himself, as he had vowed, to vindicate Silva's honour.

Macbeth, opera in four acts, with text by F. M. Piave after Shakespeare. First performed on 14 March 1847 at Teatro della Pergola, Florence; revised version on 21 April 1865 at Théâtre-Lyrique, Paris. The opera sticks closely to the outline of Shakespeare's tragedy.

Luisa Miller, opera in three acts with text by S. Cammarano based on Schiller's play *Intrigue and Love*. First performed on 8 December 1849 at Teatro San Carlo, Naples. Set in early seventeenth-century Tyrol.

Luisa (soprano), daughter of Miller (baritone), a retired soldier, has fallen in love with Carlo, a young man whose real name is Rodolfo (tenor). Rodolfo is the son of Count Walter (bass), who wishes him to marry the Duchess Federica (mezzo-soprano). In order to free her father, who has been arrested, Luisa writes a letter dictated by Wurm (bass), the Count's employee, in which she confesses her love for Wurm. Rodolfo, finding the letter, poisons both Luisa and himself. When she knows that she is dying, Luisa admits that the letter was false; she loves only Rodolfo.

Rigoletto, opera in three acts with text by F. M. Piave based on Victor Hugo's play *Le Roi s'amuse*. First performed on 11 March 1851 at Teatro la Fenice, Venice. Set in sixteenth-century Mantua.

Rigoletto (baritone), hunchback jester to the Duke of Mantua (tenor), is cursed by Monterone (baritone), whose daughter the Duke has seduced. Rigoletto's own daughter, Gilda (soprano), unaware of her father's occupation, has fallen in love with a young student—the Duke incognito—who follows her home from church and bribes her nurse Giovanna (mezzo-soprano) to let him into the garden of Rigoletto's house. Meanwhile the courtiers plan to abduct the girl, whom they believe to be Rigoletto's mistress, and present her to the Duke. Rigoletto himself, blindfolded, unwittingly aids the kidnappers. He swears vengeance on the Duke for having seduced Gilda, and hires Sparafucile (bass), an assassin, to kill him. Even the sight of her lover flirting with Maddalena (contralto), Sparafucile's sister, does not alter Gilda's love for the Duke, and she allows herself to be killed in his place. Rigoletto, opening the sack that contains the body of his victim, finds the dying Gilda inside.

Il trovatore (The Troubadour), opera in four acts with text by S. Cammarano based on a play by A. G. Gutierrez. First performed on 19 January 1853 at Teatro Apollo, Rome. Set in Biscay and Aragon in the fifteenth century.

ACT 1. Ferrando (bass), a captain in Count di Luna's army, relates how, many years ago, the Count's baby brother was bewitched by a gypsy. The gypsy was burned as a witch, but her daughter kidnapped the child and the skeleton of a baby was later found in the ashes.

Leonora (soprano), lady-in-waiting to the Princess of Aragon, listens for a Troubadour (tenor) who comes to serenade her, and with whom she is in love. Count di

VERDI

Luna (baritone), who loves Leonora, approaches her window, where a light burns. Hearing the Troubadour's song, Leonora runs out into the garden, at first mistaking Luna for her lover. Luna challenges the Troubadour, who reveals his identity as Manrico, a rebel under sentence of death. The two men fight a duel.

ACT 2. In the gypsy encampment, Manrico recovers from a wound received in battle. He is cared for by Azucena (mezzo-soprano), whom he thinks is his mother. Azucena, the daughter of the gypsy burned to death by the old Count di Luna, tells him her version of the story. With her own baby in her arms, she had watched her mother die, then kidnapped Luna's baby son and, to avenge her mother, in a passion had thrown him on the fire. But afterwards she found that it was her own child that she had mistakenly killed. Manrico is horrified and Azucena denies the story, which is in fact the truth. News is brought that Leonora, believing Manrico dead, is about to enter a convent.

In the courtyard of the convent, Luna, Ferrando and their men hide, intending to kidnap Leonora. They are disturbed by the sudden arrival of Manrico and his followers. In the ensuing fight, Manrico wins and leaves with Leonora.

ACT 3. Azucena has been found near Luna's camp and is brought before the Count. Ferrando recognizes her as the gypsy responsible for the death of the Count's brother and, when she calls on Manrico to save her, Luna realizes that she is the Troubadour's mother.

In the castle of Castellor, Leonora and Manrico are about to be married when news of the capture of Azucena reaches Manrico. He summons his men and goes off to save his mother.

ACT 4. Manrico has been captured by Luna, and is held in a tower of the palace. Monks sing a Miserere for the prisoner, who is to be executed at dawn. Leonora offers herself to Luna as payment for Manrico's freedom.

Inside the tower, Manrico comforts Azucena. Leonora comes to tell Manrico that he can go free. Guessing the price to be paid, he refuses and curses her. Leonora, who has swallowed poison rather than submit to Luna, dies in Manrico's arms. Luna has Manrico taken to execution and forces Azucena to watch. 'He was your brother,' she tells him. Her mother is avenged.

La traviata (literally: The Frail One), opera in three acts with text by F. M. Piave based on the play *La Dame aux camélias* by A. Dumas fils. First performed on 6 March 1853 at Teatro la Fenice, Venice. Set in contemporary Paris and its environs.

ACT 1. At a party given by the courtesan Violetta Valéry (soprano), Alfredo Germont (tenor), a young man who has long admired her from a distance, declares his love to her. At first she laughs at him, but his sincerity impresses her and she gives him leave to visit her again the following day.

ACT 2. Violetta has given up her hectic life in Paris and is living with Alfredo in the country. Alfredo, discovering that Violetta is about to sell her possessions to pay for their love-nest, goes to Paris to raise money himself. In his absence, Giorgio Germont (baritone), Alfredo's father, comes to ask Violetta to give up his son for the sake of his daughter, whose marriage is compromised. Violetta, though aware that she has not long to live, reluctantly agrees.

Violetta, who has returned to her former protector, Baron Douphol (bass), and Alfredo arrive separately at a party given by Flora Bervoix (mezzo-soprano). Alfredo wins a great deal of money from the Baron at cards and then throws it in Violetta's face as payment of his debt to her.

ACT 3. Violetta, abandoned by everyone but her maid Annina (soprano) and Doctor Grenvil (bass), is dying of consumption. Alfredo, who fought a duel with the Baron and then went abroad, has been told the truth of her renunciation and returns with his father. But it is too late; after a rapturous reunion with Alfredo, Violetta dies.

Simon Boccanegra, opera in prologue and three acts with text by F. M. Piave. First performed on 12 March 1857 at Teatro la Fenice, Venice; revised version, with text revised by A. Boito, produced on 24 March 1881 at La Scala, Milan. Set in Genoa in the mid-fourteenth century.

PROLOGUE. Simon Boccanegra (baritone), a buccaneer, incurs the enmity of Jacopo Fiesco (bass), a patrician, by seducing his daughter Maria. Boccanegra is elected Doge, but the death of Maria and the disappearance of their daughter make the honour an empty one.

ACT 1. Twenty-five years have passed. Fiesco, under the name of Andrea, and Gabriele Adorno (tenor), a young patrician, are plotting against the Doge. Boccanegra brings Amelia Grimaldi (soprano) a pardon for her exiled brothers. Amelia, who is in love with Adorno, complains to the Doge of the attentions of Paolo (baritone), his henchman. She is not a Grimaldi, but an adopted child, she tells Boccanegra, showing him a locket with a portrait of her mother. It is identical to the one he wears round his own neck—Amelia is his long-lost daughter.

In the council chamber a debate on the proposed war against Venice is interrupted by the intrusion of a crowd headed by Adorno. He has killed a ruffian who was attempting to kidnap Amelia and, assuming Boccanegra to be behind the plot, comes to challenge him. Amelia interrupts the scene. She knows that Paolo was behind the kidnapping but, before she can say so, the patrician and plebeian councillors start fighting.

Boccanegra appeals for peace and then forces Paolo to curse the villain—himself.

ACT 2. In the Doge's apartment, Paolo poisons the water-jug. He then tells Adorno, who is in protective custody, that Amelia is Boccanegra's mistress. When Adorno accuses Amelia of infidelity, she denies it, but admits to loving Boccanegra. On the Doge's entry, Adorno hides. Boccanegra drinks the poisoned water and falls asleep. Adorno emerges and is about to kill the Doge when Amelia stops him. Boccanegra wakes and reveals the truth: Amelia is his daughter. Adorno, overcome with remorse, is pardoned and goes to try and avert the patrician uprising.

ACT 3. The plebians have overcome the rebels. Paolo is led to execution, first confessing to Fiesco his guilt and revenge on Boccanegra. The Doge, already dying, greets Fiesco with joy. Now that he has found Fiesco's granddaugher, Boccanegra can be forgiven. He blesses Amelia and Adorno, who have just celebrated their wedding, nominates Adorno as Doge, and dies in peace.

Un ballo in maschera (A Masked Ball), opera in three acts with text by A. Somma based on *Gustave III ou le Bal masqué*, a libretto by Scribe, originally written for Auber. First performed on 17 February 1859 at Teatro Apollo, Rome. Owing to censorship difficulties, the setting was changed from eighteenth-century Stockholm to seventeenth-century Boston. The Swedish settings and characters are sometimes used.

ACT 1. Riccardo, Count of Warwick and Governor of Boston (tenor), is warned by his secretary Renato (baritone) about a plot against his life. The Chief Justice (tenor) asks the Count to sign an order for banishment against a fortune-teller, Ulrica, but Oscar (soprano), Riccardo's page, pleads on her behalf and Riccardo invites the courtiers to accompany him, in disguise, to visit the fortune-teller.

In her hut, Ulrica (contralto) summons the prince of darkness. Riccardo, dressed as a fisherman, arrives in time to hear Amelia (soprano), Renato's wife, consult Ulrica for a remedy to overcome her love for Riccardo. Ulrica suggests a magic herb that grows only at the foot of the gallows. Oscar and the courtiers arrive in disguise, and Riccardo has his fortune told. Ulrica claims that he will soon be murdered, by the next man to shake his hand. Just then Renato arrives and takes it. Ulrica repeats her warning, as the people, who have recognized the Count, sing his praises.

ACT 2. At midnight Amelia seeks the magic herb under the gallows. Riccardo has followed her and passionately declares his love. Amelia put down her veil as Renato comes to warn Riccardo that the conspirators have followed him. The two men exchange cloaks and Renato swears to escort the veiled lady back to the city without asking her identity. The conspirators, headed by Samuel and Tom (basses), are surprised to find Renato instead of the Count, and demand to know who the lady is. To prevent bloodshed, Amelia unveils herself and the conspirators taunt Renato for having an assignation with his own wife.

ACT 3. Renato threatens to kill Amelia, and she begs to be allowed to see her son first. Renato reflects that Riccardo, not Amelia, is the real culprit. When Samuel and Tom arrive to see him, he demands to join their conspiracy which, he assures them, he knows all about. The three men decide to draw lots for the honour of killing Riccardo. Amelia comes to announce Oscar and she is forced to pick the name: it is Renato. Oscar brings an invitation to a masked ball that evening.

Riccardo decides that Renato and Amelia must return to England. Oscar brings him an unsigned note warning him not to attend the masked ball, but he thinks only of seeing Amelia once more.

At the ball, Renato tricks Oscar into disclosing Riccardo's costume. Riccardo and Amelia meet and are bidding each other farewell as Renato stabs the Count. Everyone unmasks. Riccardo swears to Renato that Amelia has not betrayed him, and shows him the order for their return to England. After pardoning the conspirators, Riccardo dies.

La forza del destino (The Force of Destiny), opera in four acts with text by F. M. Piave based on a play by the Duke of Rivas. First performed on 10 November 1862 at the Imperial Theatre, St Petersburg; revised version on 20 February 1869 at La Scala, Milan. Set in Spain and Italy during the mid-eighteenth century.

The Marquis of Calatrava (bass) is accidentally killed by Don Alvaro (tenor) during Alvaro's elopement with Leonora (soprano), the Marquis's daughter. Separated during their flight and each thinking the other dead, Leonora takes refuge in a cave near the monastery of Hornachuelos and Alvaro joins the army, under another name. Meanwhile the Marquis's son, Don Carlo (baritone), swears vengeance on them both. Losing track of Leonora, he too joins the army under an assumed name. Near Velletri, in Italy, he meets Alvaro, who saves his life and is then wounded. Carlo, his suspicions aroused, discovers a portrait of Leonora in the other's possession. When Alvaro has recovered, Carlo challenges him to a duel. Soldiers separate them and Alvaro returns to Spain and becomes a monk at Hornachuelos. Carlo traces him there and again challenges him to fight, goading him with insults until he agrees. Carlo is wounded in the duel and Alvaro goes to Leonora's cave for a priest to give the dying man absolution. Leonora and Alvaro recognize each other with amazement. Learning that her brother is wounded, Leonora runs to him. With his final strength he stabs her. The Father Superior (bass) calls on Alvaro to submit to God's will and Leonora dies tranquilly.

Don Carlos, opera in five acts with text (in French) by J. Méry and C. du Locle based on the play by Schiller. First performed on 11 March 1867 at the Paris Opéra; revised version in four acts (in Italian) on 10 January 1884 at La Scala, Milan. Set in France and Spain during 1568.

ACT 1. Don Carlos (tenor), son of King Philip II of Spain, is betrothed to Elisabeth de Valois (soprano), daughter of Henry II of France, and meets her in the forest of Fontainebleau, where they express their mutual love. News is brought that Philip, to end the war between France and Spain, will marry Elisabeth himself. (This act is omitted in the Italian version.)

ACT 2. At the monastery of San Yuste, Carlos admits to his friend, the Marquis di Posa (baritone), that he loves Elisabeth, who is now his stepmother. With Posa's help, Carlos obtains an audience with the Queen. He declares his love but she sends him away. King Philip (bass), annoyed to find the Queen unattended, dismisses her lady-in-waiting. He asks Posa why he has never sought royal favour. Posa appeals to Philip to permit a less cruel and oppressive rule in Flanders.

Carlos meets a veiled lady in the Queen's gardens in Madrid. Under the impression that she is Elisabeth, he tells her of his love. But she is Princess Eboli (mezzo-soprano), a lady-in-waiting to the Queen and herself in love with Carlos. Realizing that Carlos has mistaken her for Elisabeth, she threatens to tell the King. Posa asks Carlos to give him any incriminating documents in his possession.

ACT 3. Outside the cathedral the crowd waits to see the heretics condemned by the Inquisition burned in an auto-da-fe. As the King makes his appearance, Carlos leads in a deputation from Flanders; they kneel and beg for mercy for their country. The King refuses. When

Carlos demands the governorship of Flanders for himself and draws his sword, the King calls for his son's arrest. No one dares obey until Posa steps forward and asks for Carlos's sword. The auto-da-fe continues.

ACT 4. Philip, deploring the isolation of a monarch, asks the Grand Inquisitor (bass) for advice on how to deal with his son. The Inquisitor demands death for Carlos and also for Posa, who is a danger to the Church with his liberal ideas. When Elisabeth complains that her casket of jewels has been stolen, Philip points to it on his desk. He opens it and inside finds a miniature of Carlos. Elisabeth's excuse that she was once betrothed to Carlos is dismissed, and the King calls her an adulteress. Eboli confesses to the Queen that not only did she give the casket to Philip, but that she had been his mistress. Elisabeth gives her one day either to enter a convent or leave the country. Eboli vows that she will use that day to save Carlos.

Posa visits Carlos in prison. The documents relating to the Flanders rebellion have been found in Posa's possession and he is shot by order of the Inquisition. Before he dies, Posa tells Carlos that Elisabeth will meet him at San Yuste. Phillip enters with his court and the crowd surges in to demand Carlos's freedom. Eboli, in disguise, urges Carlos to escape, as the Grand Inquisitor orders the rebels to their knees.

ACT 5. In San Yuste, Elisabeth waits to say goodbye to Carlos. Their farewells are interrupted by the King and the Grand Inquisitor, who order the arrest of Carlos. But Carlos is saved by the apparition of his grandfather, Charles V (bass), whose voice Philip and the Inquisitor recognize.

Aida, opera in four acts with text by C. du Locle and A. Ghislanzoni, based on a synopsis by A. Mariette. First performed on 24 December 1871 at Cairo Opera House. Set in Memphis and Thebes during the time of the pharaohs.

ACT 1. Aida (soprano), daughter of Amonasro, King of Ethiopia, is the slave of Amneris (mezzo-soprano), daughter of the Pharaoh. She is secretly in love with Radamès (tenor), the warrior chosen to lead the Egyptians against the Ethiopians. Amneris, though she does not know Aida's real identity, suspects her of loving Radamès, whom she too loves, and tricks her slave into admitting it.

ACT 2. The victorious Radamès returns with many captive Ethiopians, among them Amonasro (baritone), who admits to being Aida's father. He is not recognized as the Ethiopian King, who is believed to have been killed. Radamès asks the Pharaoh (bass) for the captives to be freed. At the suggestion of Ramfis (bass), the high priest, Aida's father is kept as hostage. The Pharaoh bestows his daughter's hand on Radamès.

ACT 3. Aida waits to meet Radamès by the banks of the Nile. Amonasro demands that she find out which route the Egyptian troops will take, so that the Ethiopians may ambush them. When Radamès joins Aida, she insists that their only chance of happiness is to flee together to her own country. The Egyptians, Radamès reveals, will go by way of the Gorge of Napata. Radamès, realizing that he has betrayed his country, refuses to escape with Aida and her father, and allows the guards to capture him.

ACT 4. Amneris has the captive Radamès brought before her. If he renounces Aida, who escaped (though her father was killed), Amneris will ask the Pharaoh to pardon Radamès. He refuses, and Ramfis and the priests pass judgement on Radamès, finding him guilty. Amneris pleads for his life, but to no avail. Radamès is entombed below the Temple of Vulcan; he hears a noise and sees Aida, who has chosen to die there with him.

Otello, opera in four acts with text by Arrigo Boito

based on Shakespeare's *Othello*; first performed on 5 February 1887 at La Scala, Milan. Boito stays very close to Shakespeare in his version of the tragedy, but he dispenses with the early scenes in Venice as well as the character of Brabantio, father to Desdemona, and sets the whole opera in Cyprus.

Falstaff, opera in three acts with text by Boito based on Shakespeare's comedy *The Merry Wives of Windsor*; first performed on 9 February 1893 at La Scala, Milan. Boito cut *The Merry Wives* very considerably in his libretto, dispensing with several characters, including Master Page, and transferring his daughter Anne to Master and Mistress Ford. Falstaff is also given some remarks derived from *Henry IV*.

Wagner, Richard (1813–83), German composer. His first opera to be completed, *Die Feen* (The Fairies), was not performed until 1888, five years after the composer's death. *Das Liebesverbot* (The Ban on Love), with text by the composer derived from Shakespeare's *Measure for Measure*, received a single performance in 1836 at Magdeburg. With *Rienzi* (1842), an adaptation of Bulwer Lytton's novel *Rienzi* or *The Last of the Tribunes*, Wagner scored some success at the Dresden Court Opera. *Der fliegende Holländer* (1843) and *Tannhäuser* (1845), at the same theatre, were not initially successful, though *Tannhäuser* soon became popular. Meanwhile, Wagner, because of his support for the 1849 Revolution in Dresden, had to leave Saxony and take up residence in Switzerland. *Lohengrin*, produced in 1850 at Weimar, with Liszt as conductor, was the last new Wagner opera staged for 15 years.

After an attempt to conquer Paris with a revised version of *Tannhäuser* (1861) that received three performances at the Opéra, Wagner endeavoured to produce *Tristan und Isolde* (completed in 1859) at the

Vienna Court Opera, but after a long period of rehearsal the production was cancelled. The composer was at the nadir of his fortunes when Ludwig II of Bavaria, who had just succeeded to the throne, summoned him to Munich, where *Tristan und Isolde* (1865), *Die Meistersinger von Nürnberg* (1868), *Rheingold* (1869) and *Die Walküre* (1870) were all first produced. *Siegfried* and *Götterdämmerung* (1876), the third and fourth operas in *Der Ring des Nibelungen*, and *Parsifal* (1882), were first produced at Bayreuth in the theatre built by Wagner to stage his works under festival conditions.

Der fliegende Holländer (The Flying Dutchman), opera in three acts with text by the composer, based on Heine's *Memoirs of Herr von Schnabelewopski*. First performed on 2 January 1843 at the Dresden Hofoper. Set on the coast of Norway in the eighteenth century.

ACT 1. A Dutch sea-captain, condemned for blasphemy to sail for ever, comes ashore every seven years to search for a woman willing to love and die for him, thus lifting the sentence. The Dutchman's vessel anchors in a bay where another ship, captained by Daland (bass), is sheltering from a storm. The Dutchman (baritone), learning that Daland has a daughter, asks if he can marry her, offering Daland a rich hoard of treasure in return for a night's lodging. The wind veers to the south and both ships proceed to the fishing village where Daland lives.

ACT 2. In Daland's house the women are spinning. His daughter Senta (soprano) gazes at a portrait of the Flying Dutchman hanging on the wall. The other girls tease her, and she sings them a ballad about the wretched wanderer. Erik (tenor), a huntsman, brings news that Daland's ship has been sighted. Erik, who is in love with Senta, tells her of a dream in which he saw her father come ashore from a ghostly vessel with the man from the portrait, whom Senta greeted with

(*right*) Verdi *La traviata*. English National Opera, 1974. Violetta (Valerie Masterson)

(*below*) Verdi *Un ballo in maschera*. Royal Opera Covent Garden, 1975. Amelia (Katia Ricciarelli), Gustavo (Placido Domingo) (Donald Southern)

(*above*) Verdi *Simon Boccanegra*. Royal Opera Covent Garden, 1980. Amelia (Kiri Te Kanawa), Fiesco (Robert Lloyd), Boccanegra (Sherill Milnes), Adorno (Veriano Luchetti) (Zoë Dominic)

(*right*) Verdi *Otello*. English National Opera, 1981. Otello (Charles Craig) (Reg Wilson)

Wagner *Lohengrin*. Royal Opera Covent Garden, 1977. Elsa (Anna Tomova-Sintov), Lohengrin (René Kollo), and full cast (Zoë Dominic)

(*above*) Wagner *Die Meistersinger von Nürnberg*. Deutsche Staatsoper, East Berlin, 1968. Hans Sachs (Theo Adam)

(*below*) Weber *Der Freischütz*. Royal Opera Covent Garden, 1978. Aennchen (Lucia Popp), Agathe (Hannelore Bode), Cuno (Richard Van Allan) (Donald Southern)

rapture. When Daland and the Dutchman arrive, Senta, instantly recognizing the stranger, gazes at him, silent and motionless. After urging his daughter to consider marrying the stranger, Daland goes out. Senta assures the Dutchman that she will bring him salvation through her love; she understands the sacrifice that will be required of her.

ACT 3. On the quayside the Norwegian seamen drink and dance with their girls. The Dutchman's ship is unlit and deathly quiet. When, at last, ghostly voices are heard from on board, the Norwegians run away in terror. Erik accuses Senta of breaking the promise that she had made to marry him. The Dutchman, overhearing this, believes that he has been betrayed once more. Senta protests her faithfulness but the Dutchman boards his ship, which sets sail. Senta tears herself away from Erik and leaps into the sea. The Dutchman's ship sinks immediately, its Captain redeemed by the love of a woman faithful unto death.

Tannhäuser, opera in three acts with text by the composer, first performed on 19 October 1845 at the Dresden Hofoper; revised version on 13 March 1861 at the Paris Opéra. Set in Thuringia early in the thirteenth century.

ACT 1. Tannhäuser (tenor), a knight and minstrel, has been lured by Venus (soprano) to her court inside the Venusberg, where she entertains him with a bacchanal. But Tannhäuser, surfeited of pleasure, invokes the Virgin and is transported to a valley below the castle of the Wartburg. A band of pilgrims files past, then Hermann (bass), Landgrave of Thuringia, out hunting with his knights, recognizes Tannhäuser and invites him back to the castle for the Song Contest. Tannhäuser refuses until one of the knights, Wolfram von Eschenbach (baritone), mentions Elisabeth, the niece of the Landgrave.

ACT 2. Elisabeth (soprano) greets Tannhäuser in the Hall of Song. Guests and singers assemble for the contest and the Landgrave offers the hand of his niece to the winner. The theme of the contest is Love. Wolfram sings of chaste, courtly love and is followed by Tannhäuser, who praises the delights of carnal love. Biterolf (bass) accuses Tannhäuser of blasphemy. Wolfram again sings of spiritual love, then Tannhäuser breaks out into a wild hymn to Venus. The knights draw their swords in anger but Elisabeth pleads for mercy on Tannhäuser's behalf. The Landgrave gives judgement: Tannhäuser must join the pilgrim band on its way to Rome.

ACT 3. Elisabeth and Wolfram wait in the valley below the Wartburg as the pilgrims return from Rome. Tannhäuser is not among them. Elisabeth offers a prayer to the Virgin, then returns to the castle. As it grows dark, Tannhäuser appears. He tells Wolfram that the Pope rejected his plea for forgiveness; he is accursed until the papal staff sprouts new leaves, and intends to return to the Venusberg. Wolfram invokes the name of Elisabeth as a funeral procession descends from the Wartburg, carrying her body. Tannhäuser sinks dying on the corpse while pilgrims arrive with the Pope's staff, which is bearing fresh green leaves.

Lohengrin, opera in three acts with text by the composer, first performed on 28 August 1850 at Weimar Hoftheater. Set in Antwerp in the tenth century.

ACT 1. Godfrey, heir to the dukedom of Brabant, has disappeared. His sister Elsa (soprano) is accused of murdering him by Frederick of Telramund (baritone) and his wife Ortrud (mezzo-soprano). Henry the Fowler (bass), King of Germany, who is in Antwerp to raise an army to fight against the Hungarians, rules that the dispute be settled by combat between Frederick and a knight representing Elsa. Elsa describes a knight that she saw in a dream, and the Herald (baritone) summons him. After a further summons, a boat drawn by a swan is sighted on the river Scheldt, and Lohengrin (tenor) steps ashore. As Elsa's champion, he asks her to marry him, on the condition that she does not try to discover his name. Elsa joyfully agrees and the Knight defeats Frederick, who is exiled by the King.

ACT 2. On the steps of the minster, Ortrud and Frederick plot the downfall of Elsa and her Knight. Ortrud insinuates herself into the castle by evoking Elsa's sympathy. The bridal procession enters but is halted by Ortrud and Frederick, who throw doubt on the Knight's motive in concealing his identity. Lohengrin comes to Elsa's help and the procession continues to the minster.

ACT 3. Alone with him after the wedding ceremony, Elsa is consumed with desire to know her champion's name, and finally she asks him outright. At that moment Frederick, with four of his followers, bursts into the room. Lohengrin strikes him dead with his sword and orders the others to remove the body. He will answer Elsa's question the next morning.

The King and the Brabantine nobles gather by the river. Lohengrin cannot now lead them into battle, but he prophesies their victory. To Elsa he announces his name—Lohengrin, son of Parsifal, and Knight of the Holy Grail. The swan reappears and Lohengrin is about to leave when Ortrud claims that the swan is Godfrey, transformed by her magic. Lohengrin kneels down in prayer, a dove descends to draw the boat, the swan vanishes and in its place stands Godfrey. Elsa falls dead in her brother's arms as Lohengrin departs.

Tristan und Isolde, opera in three acts with text by the composer, first performed on 10 June 1865 at Munich Hof- und Nationaltheater.

ACT 1. Tristan (tenor), nephew of the Cornish king, Mark, is escorting the Irish princess Isolde (soprano) by ship to Cornwall, as bride to his uncle. Isolde tells her attendant Brangäne (mezzo-soprano) how Tristan had killed Morold, her betrothed. Tristan, badly wounded in the fight, came to Isolde, noted for her skill in healing, under the name of Tantris. Although she recognized him, she cured his wound, for which he professed eternal gratitude. Now she curses him as a traitor for delivering her to a loveless marriage. Brangäne reminds her mistress of the casket of magic potions that Isolde carries. Kurwenal (baritone), Tristan's retainer, announces their imminent arrival. Isolde demands to speak to Tristan. She instructs Brangäne to prepare the death potion. To Tristan she declares that he must atone for the death of Morold. They drink the potion from the cup, expecting to die, but Brangäne has substituted the love potion. Tristan and Isolde fall ecstatically into each other's arms, the love that they have been hiding in their hearts released.

ACT 2. King Mark (bass) has gone hunting and Isolde extinguishes the torch outside her apartment as a signal to Tristan. They express their love in rapturous phrases. Brangäne, keeping watch in the tower, warns them that day approaches, and they yearn for eternal night. At the height of their transports the King's party returns, headed by Melot (tenor), who has betrayed the lovers. Mark expresses his pain and sorrow at Tristan's disloyalty. Tristan, first asking Isolde to accompany him to the land of night, falls on Melot's sword.

ACT 3. In Kareol, Tristan's Breton castle, Kurwenal watches over his unconscious master. A Shepherd (tenor) plays a mournful tune on his pipe. When a ship is sighted, he will play a brighter melody. Tristan wakes and, learning that Kurwenal has sent for Isolde, who will cure his wound as she did before, becomes overwrought. In his delirium he imagines he sees the ship, but the Shepherd plays the same sad strain. At last the Piper breaks into a merry tune. While Kurwenal goes to meet Isolde, Tristan feverishly tears the bandage from his wound. When Isolde appears he falls dead in her arms. After chiding him for preceding her in death, she sinks unconscious. The Shepherd informs Kurwenal that another ship has been sighted, with King Mark on board. Kurwenal and other retainers seek to barricade the castle; Kurwenal kills Melot and is himself mortally wounded before King Mark and Brangäne enter. Brangäne has told the King about the love potion and he comes to reunite Tristan and Isolde. Isolde awakens, but only to achieve a mystical union with Tristan in death.

Die Meistersinger von Nürnberg (The Mastersingers of Nuremberg), opera in three acts with text by the composer, first performed on 21 June 1868 at Hof- und Nationaltheater, Munich. Set in Nuremberg about 1560.

ACT 1. In St Catherine's Church a young knight, Walther von Stolzing (tenor), admires Eva (soprano), daughter of the goldsmith Pogner. Her nurse, Magdalena (mezzo-soprano), informs Walther that Eva is to marry the winner of the Mastersingers' contest. David (tenor), apprentice to the shoemaker Hans Sachs, instructs Walther in the complicated rules of mastersinging, as his fellow apprentices arrange the church for a trial. Pogner (bass), Hans Sachs (bass-baritone) and the other Masters enter, and Pogner announces his decision to give Eva as a prize to the winner of the song contest. Walther presents himself as a candidate for trial and sings in praise of love, but Sextus Beckmesser (bass), the town clerk, who acts as marker, and the other Masters are shocked by the novelty of his song. Only Sachs finds it interesting.

ACT 2. In the street outside his house, on midsummer eve, Sachs works on a pair of shoes. Eva, who lives opposite, is upset to hear that Walther has failed the trial. When Sachs has gone into his workshop, Eva meets Walther. If he cannot become a Master they will have to elope. But another suitor arrives to serenade Eva—Beckmesser. While Magdalena sits in her window, Eva and Walther hide behind a lime tree and Sachs resumes his cobbling, singing loudly as he works. Beckmesser's serenade, 'marked' by Sachs with a hammer on the shoe-sole, arouses the neighbours. In the ensuing confusion Sachs sends Eva home and takes Walther into his own house. When the Watchman (bass) calls eleven, the street is deserted.

ACT 3. In Sachs's workshop, early on midsummer's day, Walther relates a dream he has just had and Sachs writes it down as a prize song for the knight to sing in the contest. As they go off to put on their best clothes, Beckmesser comes in; he is astonished to see a prize song in Sachs's handwriting. The shoemaker gives Beckmesser the song, assuring him that, although he is a widower, he does not intend to take part in the contest. Eva, under the pretext that her shoes do not fit, arrives to see Walther, followed by Magdalena and David. Sachs christens Walther's prize song 'The Morning Dream's Interpretation'.

Outside the town the people gather for the contest. The Mastersingers take their places, with Eva in the seat of honour. Sachs is warmly welcomed by the crowd. Beckmesser sings first and, trying to fit Walther's words, which he remembers wrongly, to the tune of his previous night's serenade, is laughed at by the assembly. He accuses Sachs of having written the song, but Sachs calls the real author. Walther steps forward and wins the contest with his prize song. Eva presents him with a laurel crown, but when Pogner offers him the insignia of a Mastersinger, Walther refuses it. Sachs, in a tribute to German art, reproves the knight, who then accepts the chain and title of Mastersinger.

Das Rheingold (The Rhinegold), prologue, in four scenes, to *Der Ring des Nibelungen* (The Nibelung's Ring), with text by the composer; first performed on 22 September 1869 at Hof- und Nationaltheater, Munich.

Alberich (bass-baritone), the Nibelung dwarf, has stolen the Rhinemaidens' gold and, by renouncing love, forges it into a Ring that gives him unlimited power. Wotan (bass-baritone), chief of the gods, has promised to give Freia (soprano), goddess of Youth and Beauty, to the giants Fasolt and Fafner (basses) as payment for building his castle, Valhalla. He learns about the Ring from Loge (tenor), god of Fire, whom he has asked to find an alternative payment for the giants. Descending into Nibelheim with Loge, Wotan captures Alberich and his gold by a trick. Alberich curses the Ring. The giants accept the gold in place of Freia, but demand the Ring as well. Wotan at first refuses to part with it, but Erda (contralto), the Earth goddess, advises him to relinquish it. Alberich's curse claims its first victim when Fafner kills Fasolt to gain possession of the Ring. As Wotan leads his wife Fricka (mezzo-soprano) and the other gods across a rainbow bridge to Valhalla, the Rhinemaidens (two sopranos, one mezzo-soprano) are heard calling for the return of their gold.

Die Walküre (The Valkyrie), opera in three acts; second part of *The Nibelung's Ring*, with text by the composer. First performed on 26 June 1870 at Hof- und Nationaltheater, Munich.

ACT 1. Wotan, in order to father a hero to regain the Ring for him, descends to Earth and begets the Wälsung twins, Siegmund (tenor) and Sieglinde (soprano), who are separated in childhood. Siegmund, fleeing from his enemies, takes shelter in the dwelling of Hunding (bass), whose wife Sieglinde feels an instant attraction for the fugitive. Hunding discovers that Siegmund has killed many of his kinsfolk and challenges him to fight. While her husband lies in a drugged sleep, Sieglinde shows Siegmund a sword in the central ash-tree of the dwelling. It belongs to the man who can draw it out. Siegmund draws the sword, and brother and sister, rapturously greeting each other by name, rush out into the night.

ACT 2. The Earth goddess, Erda, has borne Wotan a daughter, Brünnhilde (soprano). With her Valkyrie sisters she carries dead heroes to Valhalla. Brünnhilde is to shield Siegmund in the coming fight, but Fricka, as protector of the marriage vow, insists that Hunding, not Siegmund, must win and that Wotan alter his instructions to Brünnhilde accordingly. As Sieglinde sleeps, exhausted, Brünnhilde appears to Siegmund to announce his death. Siegmund's grief at parting from Sieglinde is so extreme that Brünnhilde decides to disobey her orders. Hunding and Siegmund fight. Brünnhilde protects Siegmund, but Wotan appears and Siegmund's sword shatters, as Hunding kills him. Brünnhilde gathers up the sword fragments and leads the bewildered Sieglinde away.

ACT 3. Brünnhilde's eight sister-Valkyries assemble on a rock. Brünnhilde arrives with Sieglinde and, telling her that she will bear Siegmund's child, gives her the sword fragments. She sends her into the forest where Fafner, in the shape of a dragon, guards the Nibelung treasure. Wotan arrives and, dismissing the other Valkyries, informs Brünnhilde of her punishment. She will be put to sleep on the rock for the first man who comes along to waken and make his slave. Brünnhilde protests that she only carried out Wotan's secret wish in protecting his son. She persuades her father to ring the rock with fire so that only the bravest hero will get through the flames to wake her. Wotan kisses her farewell, covers her with her shield and then summons Loge.

Siegfried, opera in three acts; third part of *The Nibelung's Ring*, with text by the composer. First performed on 16 August 1876 at Bayreuth.

ACT 1. Mime (tenor), brother to Alberich, sheltered Sieglinde in his cave and, after she died in childbirth, brought up her son Siegfried (tenor). He plans to use Siegfried to kill the dragon Fafner and so obtain the Nibelung gold, but he cannot reforge the sword fragments. Wotan, disguised as the Wanderer, tells Mime that the sword will be forged by one who knows no fear and that the dwarf's head will be forfeit to that person. Mime tries in vain to teach fear to Siegfried. Learning that the sword fragments belonged to his father, Siegfried reforges them himself, while Mime brews a poisonous drink.

ACT 2. Outside Fafner's cave, the Wanderer warns Alberich that his brother plans to steal the Nibelung gold. Mime shows Siegfried the Dragon's lair. A Woodbird sings in the trees above and Siegfried tries to imitate its song, first on a reed-pipe, then on his horn. The sound wakes Fafner, who emerges from his cave and is killed by Siegfried. Retrieving his sword, Siegfried is burned by a drop of Dragon's blood and, putting his hand to his mouth, he begins to understand the Woodbird (soprano). She tells him to take the Ring and the Tarnhelm, a magic mask, from the cave, then warns him against Mime, who intends to give him a sleeping potion and then cut off his head. Siegfried kills the dwarf and Alberich's mocking laughter is heard. The Woodbird tells Siegfried that a bride awaits him on the Valkyrie rock.

ACT 3. Wotan summons Erda, but she has no advice for him. Siegfried, led by the Woodbird, approaches.

He is impatient when the Wanderer bars his way and, learning that the old man's spear once shattered his sword, resulting in his father's death, he in his turn shatters the spear, and with it the god's power.

The flames leap up round the Valkyrie rock, but Siegfried passes safely through them, to find a sleeping figure. Removing shield, helmet and breastplate, he discovers a woman, the first he has seen, and at last he learns to fear. He awakens Brünnhilde with a kiss. She greets him joyfully at first, but then is reluctant to surrender herself. Siegfried's love overcomes her scruples and she falls into his arms.

Götterdämmerung (The Twilight of the Gods), opera in prologue and three acts; fourth part of *The Nibelung's Ring*, with text by the composer. First performed on 17 August 1876 at Bayreuth; first complete cycle of *The Nibelung's Ring* performed on 13, 14, 16, and 17 August 1876 at Bayreuth.

PROLOGUE. The rope of destiny, woven by three Norns (contralto, mezzo-soprano and soprano), breaks. On the Valkyrie rock Siegfried says goodbye to Brünnhilde; he gives her the Ring and she gives him her horse, Grane.

ACT 1. In the Hall of the Gibichungs on the Rhine, Gunther (baritone) and his sister Gutrune (soprano) are told by their half-brother Hagen (bass), a son of Alberich, of suitable spouses. Siegfried the Hero will win Brünnhilde for Gunther, who can give him Gutrune as bride in return. Siegfried's horn is heard from the Rhine, and Hagen calls to him to land. A magic potion makes Siegfried forget Brünnhilde and fall in love with Gutrune. He swears blood-brotherhood with Gunther and agrees to win Gunther's bride for him by means of the Tarnhelm, which will transform Siegfried into the likeness of Gunther. Hagen is left to guard the Gibichung Hall.

On her rock, Brünnhilde waits for Siegfried's return. One of the Valkyries, Waltraute (mezzo-soprano), comes to inform her sister of the imminent downfall of the gods. Seeing the Ring on Brünnhilde's finger, she urges her to return it to the Rhinemaidens. But Brünnhilde will not give up Siegfried's love gift and the fate of the gods no longer concerns her. The flames spurt up but, instead of Siegfried, a stranger appears. He tears the Ring from Brünnhilde's finger and she is overpowered.

ACT 2. Alberich appears to Hagen, who promises his father that he will obtain the Ring. Siegfried, returning in his own form, is greeted by Gutrune. Hagen summons the Gibichung vassals to give Gunther and his bride a loyal welcome. Brünnhilde is amazed to see Siegfried, who acts as a stranger towards her. Noticing the Ring on his finger, she accuses him of stealing it and of betraying Gunther. Siegfried claims that he got the Ring from a dead dragon and swears on Hagen's spear that he did not betray Gunther. Brünnhilde swears that he did and, with Gunther and Hagen, plans to kill Siegfried.

ACT 3. During a hunt, Siegfried is teased by the Rhinemaidens, who demand his Ring. Hagen suggests that Siegfried should tell the story of his early life. When Siegfried asks for a drink, Hagen gives him a draught that restores his memory, and he describes how he followed the Woodbird and found the sleeping Brünnhilde on her rock. As Siegfried turns to watch two ravens—the harbingers of death—Hagen stabs him in the back and he falls dying on his shield.

Siegfried's body is carried to the Gibichung Hall, where Gutrune accuses Gunther of killing her husband. Gunther points to Hagen as the murderer and Hagen kills him, then goes to take the Ring from Siegfried's hand, but the corpse's arm rises threateningly. Brünnhilde comes forward. She understands all that has happened and instructs the vassals to build a funeral pyre. She takes the Ring from Siegfried's finger and, when the body has been placed on the pyre, mounts Grane and rides into the flames. The Rhine overflows and the Rhinemaidens regain their Ring. Hagen tries to follow and is drowned, while the flames of the pyre mount to Valhalla and destroy it, together with the power of the gods.

Parsifal, a sacred festival drama in three acts with text by the composer, first performed on 26 July 1882 at Bayreuth. Set in Spain during the Middle Ages.

ACT 1. The Holy Grail, the cup from which Jesus drank at the Last Supper, and the Spear that pierced His side, were in the keeping of Titurel and his knights at Montsalvat. Amfortas, Titurel's son, by succumbing to a beautiful enchantress, lost the Spear to the magician Klingsor, and received a wound from it that can only be healed by the Spear itself. Amfortas (baritone) is brought ointment by Kundry (soprano), a wild and enigmatic figure, to ease his sufferings. Gurnemanz (bass), an old knight, tells the younger esquires of a prophecy that the Spear will be returned to Montsalvat by a blameless fool. Parsifal (tenor), who has shot a swan with his crossbow, is chided by Gurnemanz; all living creatures are holy at Montsalvat. The youth knows neither his name nor anything about himself, though Kundry abruptly tells him that his mother is dead.

Gurnemanz takes the boy with him to the hall where the ceremony of the Grail takes place. The knights assemble and Amfortas is carried in. He consents to unveil the Grail only when Titurel (bass) implores him to do so. Parsifal watches the ceremony without understanding it and Gurnemanz turns him out of the hall.

ACT 2. In his castle Klingsor (bass) summons Kundry,

who is transformed into the enchantress who had tempted Amfortas, and orders her to seduce Parsifal, for he is the blameless fool of the prophecy.

In Klingsor's garden the youth is surrounded by the Flower Maidens. A voice calls his name—Parsifal—and he sees a beautiful woman reclining on a couch. At first he is attracted to her, but when she kisses him he feels the anguish of Amfortas's wound in his own breast and repulses her. Klingsor appears and hurls the Spear at Parsifal, but the youth catches the shaft and makes the sign of the cross with it. Klingsor's garden disappears.

ACT 3. Parsifal does not find his way back to Montsalvat with the Spear for many years. He is welcomed by Gurnemanz, who baptizes him. Then Parsifal baptizes Kundry. In the hall the knights demand that Amfortas should unveil the Grail, but he cannot bear the spiritual and physical anguish. Parsifal, arriving with the Spear, heals Amfortas's wound and then unveils the Grail as Kundry, her sin expiated, dies.

Walton, (Sir) William (born 1902), English composer. His only full-length opera, *Troilus and Cressida*, based on the poem by Chaucer, was first performed on 3 December 1954 at Covent Garden. *The Bear*, a one-act opera adapted from a short story by Chekhov, received its premiere at the 1967 Aldeburgh Festival.

Weber, Carl Maria von (1786–1826), German composer. His earlier operas include the one-act comedy *Abu Hassan* (1811), first produced in Munich. In *Der Freischütz* (1821), Weber composed the archetypal German Romantic opera, which has retained its popularity to the present day. *Euryanthe* (1823), first performed at the Kärntnertortheater, Vienna, suffered from the ineptitude of its text and many attempts have been made to provide the work with a more convincing libretto. *Oberon, or The Elf King's Oath*, with English text by J. R. Planché, was first performed on 12 April 1826 at Covent Garden. The composer, who had less than eight weeks left to live, was conductor. Because, once more, of a libretto written in a style found unacceptable by modern audiences, *Oberon* is more widely performed in German translation than in the original. *Die drei Pintos* (The Three Pintos), left unfinished in 1821, was completed by Gustav Mahler and produced in 1888 at Leipzig.

Der Freischütz (The Freeshooter), opera in three acts with text by F. Kind, first performed on 18 June 1821 at the Schauspielhaus, Berlin. Set in Bohemia in the mid-seventeenth century.

ACT 1. Max (tenor), a forester, is defeated in a shooting contest by Kilian (tenor), a peasant. To ensure that he passes a test of marksmanship that carries with it succession to Cuno (bass) as hereditary ranger and marriage to Cuno's daughter Agathe, Max agrees to mould some magic bullets in the Wolf's Glen with Caspar (bass), a forester who has sold his soul to Samiel, the Devil (speaker).

ACT 2. In Cuno's house, Agathe (soprano) anxiously awaits Max. Her cousin Aennchen (soprano) tries to divert her. Max joins Caspar at midnight in the Wolf's Glen. Together they mould seven magic bullets—six that will hit their mark and one, the seventh, that will go where Samiel wishes it.

ACT 3. Her bridesmaids come to fetch Agathe. After a hunt, during which Max uses six of his bullets, the test takes place before Prince Ottaker (baritone), who points to a dove as the target. Agathe cries out, then faints, while Caspar, who had hoped to gain Max's soul for Samiel, falls dead. Prince Ottaker banishes Max, but a Hermit (bass) pleads for the young man and the Prince pardons him.

Weill, Kurt (1900–50), German composer. Though he wrote other highly successful examples of music theatre, Weill's chief contributions to opera are *Die Dreigroschenoper*, with text by Bertolt Brecht adapted from *The Beggar's Opera*, first performed on 28 August 1928 at the Theater am Schiffbauerdamm, Berlin; and *Aufsteig und Fall der Stadt Mahagonny* (Rise and Fall of the City of Mahagonny), also with text by Brecht, first performed on 9 March 1930 at Leipzig. These two works exactly catch the spirit of Berlin in the late twenties and early thirties.

Weinberger, Jaromir (1896–1967), Czech composer. His first opera, *Shvanda the Bagpiper* (1927), scored a great success on its production in Prague and remains popular; his later works have not held a place in the repertory.

Williamson, Malcolm (born 1931), Australian composer. He has written several successful operas, including *Our Man in Havana* (1963), based on the novel by Graham Greene; *English Eccentrics* (1964), adapted from the book by Edith Sitwell; *The Happy Prince* (1965), a children's opera with text by the composer after Oscar Wilde; and *The Growing Castle* (1968), with text by the composer adapted from Strindberg's *Dream Play*.

Wolf-Ferrari, Ermanno (1876–1948), Italian composer. Several of his operas were first performed, in translation, in Germany. These include: *Le donne curiose*, or The Inquisitive Ladies (1903), and *I quattro rusteghi*, or The Four Curmudgeons (1906), based on comedies by C. Goldoni and staged in Munich; *Il segreto di Susanna* (1909), in which Susanna's secret was that she smoked; and *I gioielli della Madonna*, or The Jewels of the Madonna (1911), an excursion into the violence and sex of *verismo*, first performed in Berlin. *Sly* (1927), based on the prologue to Shakespeare's *Taming of the Shrew*, and *Il campiello*, or The Piazza (1936), another Goldoni comedy, were premiered at La Scala, Milan.

Zandonai, Riccardo (1883–1944), Italian composer. The most successful of his 13 operas were: *Francesca da Rimini* (1914), adapted from Gabriele d'Annunzio's drama, itself based on an episode from Dante's *Hell*, produced at Turin; *Giulietta e Romeo* (1922), an adaptation of Shakespeare's tragedy *Romeo and Juliet*, produced at Teatro Costanzi, Rome; and *I Cavalieri di Ekebu* (1925), based on Selma Lagerlöf's novel, *The Story of Gösta Berling*, first performed at La Scala, Milan.

Zimmermann, Bernd-Alois (1918–70), German composer. His opera *Die Soldaten* (The Soldiers), with text taken by the composer from a play by J. M. Lenz, was first performed on 15 February 1965 at Cologne. It uses every ingredient of music theatre: song, speech, taped and electronic music, as well as film, dance and mime. Several of the scenes take place simultaneously, as in Henze's *We Come to the River*.

BIBLIOGRAPHY

Beethoven, Marion M. Scott (Master Musicians), Dent
Bellini, Leslie Orrey (Master Musicians), Dent
Bellini, Vincenzo, his Life and his Operas, Herbert Weinstock, Weidenfeld & Nicolson, 1971
Berg, Alban, Mosco Carner, Duckworth, 1975
Berlioz, J. H. Elliot (Master Musicians), Dent
Bizet, Winton Dean (Master Musicians), Dent

BIBLIOGRAPHY

Britten, Benjamin, his Life and Operas, Eric Walter White, Faber, 1970
Cavalli, Jane Glover, Batsford, 1978
Debussy, Edward Lockspeiser (Master Musicians), Dent
Delius, Alan Jefferson (Master Musicians), Dent
Donizetti, Herbert Weinstock, Pantheon, 1963
Handel, Percy M. Young (Master Musicians), Dent
Janáček, Leoš, The Operas of, Erik Chisholm, Pergamon, 1971
Massenet, James Harding, Dent, 1970
Monteverdi, Denis Arnold (Master Musicians), Dent
Mozart, Eric Blom (Master Musicians), Dent
Mozart, The Complete Operas of, Charles Osborne, Gollancz, 1978
Mussorgsky, M. D. Calvocoressi (Master Musicians), Dent
Offenbach, Jacques, Charles Harding, Calder, 1980
Puccini, Mosco Carner, Duckworth, 1974
Puccini, The Complete Operas of, Charles Osborne, Gollancz, 1981
Purcell, Sir Jack Westrup (Master Musicians), Dent
Rossini, Herbert Weinstock, Oxford University Press, 1968
Smetana, John Clapham (Master Musicians), Dent
Strauss, Richard, Michael Kennedy (Master Musicians), Dent
Strauss, Richard, a Critical Study of his Operas, William Mann, Cassell, 1964
Stravinsky, Francis Routh (Master Musicians), Dent
Tchaikovsky, Edward Garden (Master Musicians), Dent
Tippett and his Operas, Eric Walter White, Hutchinson, 1979
Verdi, Dyneley Hussey (Master Musicians), Dent
Verdi, The Complete Operas of, Charles Osborne, Gollancz, 1969
Wagner, Robert L. Jacobs (Master Musicians), Dent
Wagner Nights, Ernest Newman, Putnam, 1949
Weber, Carl Maria von, John Warrack, Hamilton, 1968
Kobbé's Complete Opera Book, edited by the Earl of Harewood, Putnam, 1976
The Concise Oxford Dictionary of Opera, H. Rosenthal & J. Warrack, OUP, 1979

Index of Operas

Numbers in italic type refer to the photographs

Abbot of Drimock, The (Musgrave), 114
Abduction from the Seraglio, The, see *Entführung aus dem Serail, Die*
Abu Hassan (Weber), 179
Achille et Polyeucte (Lully), 95
Adelson e Salvini (Bellini), 18
Adriana Lecouvreur (Cilea), 59–60
Africaine, L' (Meyerbeer), 102
Agnes von Hohenstauffen (Spontini), 138
Agrippina (Handel), 77
Ägyptische Helena, Die (R. Strauss), 139
Aida (Verdi), 148, 159–160
Aiglon, L' (Honegger and Ibert), 88
Albert Herring (Britten), 43, 47–49
Alceste (Gluck), 73, 74
Alceste (Lully), 95
Alcina (Handel), 78
Alessandro (Handel), 77
Alessandro Stradella (Flotow), 69
Alfred (Arne), 13
Almira (Handel), 77
Alzira (Verdi), 148
Amahl and the Night Visitors (Menotti), 100
Amant jaloux, L' (Grétry), 77
Amelia goes to the Ball (Menotti), 100
Amico Fritz, L' (Mascagni), 96
Amore dei tre re, L' (Montemezzi), 102
Andrea Chénier (Giordano), 71–72
Angélique (Ibert), 88
Aniara (Blomdahl), 41
Anna Bolena (Donizetti), 63–64
Antigonae (Orff), 118
Antony and Cleopatra (Barber), 14
Apothecary, The see *Speciale, Lo*
Arabella (R. Strauss), 139, 142–143
Ariadne auf Naxos (R. Strauss), 139, 141–142
Ariane et Barbe-bleue (Dukas), 68
Ariodante (Handel), 78
Arlecchino (Busoni), 55
Arlesiana, L' (Cilea), 59
Armide (Gluck), 73
Armide et Renaud (Lully), 95
Aroldo (Verdi), 148

Artaxerxes (Arne), 13
Artemesia (Cavalli), 56
Ascanio (Saint-Saëns), 135
Ascanio in Alba (Mozart), 104
Atlantida, L' (Falla), 69
At the Boar's Head (Holst), 87
Attila (Verdi), 148
Aufstieg und Fall der Stadt Mahagonny (Weill), 181

Ballo in maschera, Un (Verdi), 148, 155–157, *163*
Bandits, The see *Masnadieri, I*
Ban on Love, The see *Liebesverbot, Das*
Barber of Bagdad, The see *Barbier von Bagdad, Der*
Barber of Seville, The see *Barbiere di Siviglia, Il*
Barbiere di Siviglia, Il (Paisiello), 118
Barbiere di Siviglia, Il (Rossini), *121*, 133–134
Barbier von Bagdad, Der (Cornelius), 61
Bartered Bride, The (Smetana), 137–138
Bassarids, The (Henze), 79–80
Bastien und Bastienne (Mozart), 104
Bat, The see *Fledermaus, Die*
Battaglia di Legnano, La (Verdi), 148
Bear, The (Walton), 179
Beatrice di Tenda (Bellini), 18
Béatrice et Bénédict (Berlioz), 28–29
Beggar's Opera, The (Britten), 43
Beggar's Opera, The (Pepusch), 8, 118–119, 181
Belle Hélène, La (Offenbach), 116
Benvenuto Cellini (Berlioz), 28–29
Bergère châtelaine, La (Auber), 13
Besuch der alten Dame, Der (Einem), 68
Betrothal in a Monastery (Prokofiev), 125
Betrothed, The see *Promessi sposi, I*
Bianca e Gernando (Bellini), 18
Billy Budd (Britten), 43, 49–51
Blue Monday, or 125th Street (Gershwin), 70
Bogatirs, The (Borodin), 42
Bohème, La (Leoncavallo), 93

INDEX

Boheme, La (Puccini), 86, 125–127
Bohemian Girl, The (Balfe), 14
Boris Godunov (Mussorgsky), 114–116
Boulevard Solitude (Henze), 78
Brandenburgers in Bohemia, The (Smetana), 137
Brautwahl, Die (Busoni), 55
Breasts of Tiresias, The see Mamelles de Tirésias, Les
Brief Life see Vida breve, La
Briseïs (Chabrier), 56
Burning Fiery Furnace, The (Britten), 43

Cadmus et Hermione (Lully), 95
Calisto, La (Cavalli), 56
Campiello, Il (Wolf-Ferrari), 182
Capriccio (R. Strauss), 123, 139, 143–144
Capture of Troy, The see Prise de Troie, La
Capuleti e i Montecchi, I (Bellini), 18
Cardillac (Hindemith), 82
Carmen (Bizet), 37, 38–41
Carmina Burana (Orff), 118
Castaway, The (Berkeley), 28
Castor et Pollux (Rameau), 132
Catulli Carmina (Orff), 118
Cavalieri di Ekebù, I (Zandonai), 182
Cavalleria rusticana (Mascagni), 83, 96–97
Cendrillon (Massenet), 97
Cenerentola, La (Rossini), 133, 134
Châlet, Le (Adam), 13
Cherevichki see Vakula the Smith
Cheval de bronze, Le (Auber), 14
Child and the Spells, The see Enfant et les sortilèges, L'
Cid, Der (Cornelius), 61
Cid, Le (Massenet), 97
Cinderella see Cendrillon
Cinderella see Cenerentola, La
Ciro (Cavalli), 56
Clemency of Titus, The see Clemenza di Tito, La
Clemenza di Tito, La (Mozart), 86, 113–114
Clever Girl, The see Kluge, Die
Cloak, The see Tabarro, Il
Clowns see Pagliacci
Comedy on the Bridge (Martinu), 95

Comte Ory, Le (Rossini), 133, 134–135
Comus (Arne), 13
Consul, The (Menotti), 100–101
Contes d'Hoffmann, Les (Offenbach), 116–118
Coronation of Poppaea, The see Incoronazione di Poppea, L'
Corsaro, Il (Verdi), 148
Cosa rara, Una (Martín y Soler), 96
Così fan tutte (Mozart), 85, 110–111
Crociato in Egitto, Il (Meyerbeer), 101
Crusader in Egypt, The see Crociato in Egitto, Il
Cunning Little Vixen, The (Janáček), 88, 90
Curlew River (Britten), 43
Cyrano de Bergerac (Alfano), 13

Dafne (Peri), 7
Dalibor (Smetana), 137
Dame blanche, La (Boieldieu), 42
Damnation de Faust, La (Berlioz), 29–30
Daphne (R. Strauss), 139
Dantons Tod (Einem), 68
Dardanus (Rameau), 132
Daughter of the Regiment, The see Fille du régiment, La
Day of Peace see Friedenstag
Dead City, The see Tote Stadt, Die
Death in Venice (Britten), 44, 53–55
Death of Danton see Dantons Tod
Deceptive Infidelity, The see Infedeltà delusa, L'
Decision, The (Musgrave), 114
Deidamia (Handel), 78
Dejanice (Catalani), 55
Démophoon (Cherubini), 58
Deux journées, Les (Cherubini), 58
Devil and Kate, The (Dvořák), 68
Dialogues des Carmélites, Les (Poulenc), 120
Diamants de la couronne, Les (Auber), 14
Dido and Aeneas (Purcell), 131–132
Dimitrij (Dvořák), 68
Dinner Engagement, A (Berkeley), 28
Dinorah see Pardon de Ploërmel, Le
Dissoluto punito, Il see Don Giovanni
Djamileh (Bizet), 37
Docteur Miracle, Le (Bizet), 32
Doktor Faust (Busoni), 55

185

INDEX

Domino noir, Le (Auber), 14
Don Carlos (Verdi), 149, 158–159
Don Giovanni (Mozart), 85, 96, 108–110
Donna del lago, La (Rossini), 133
Donne curiose, Le (Wolf-Ferrari), 181
Don Pasquale (Donizetti), 67–68
Don Procopio (Bizet), 32
Don Quichotte (Massenet), 97, 99–100
Dream of Scipio, The see Sogno di Scipione, Il
Dreigroschenoper, Die (Weill), 181
Drei Pintos, Die (Weber), 180
Due Foscari, I (Verdi), 148
Duke Bluebeard's Castle (Bartok), 14–15
Dumb Girl of Portici, The see Muette de Portici, La

Eaglet, The see Aiglon, L'
Edmea (Catalani), 56
Éducation manquée, Une (Chabrier), 56
Egisto, L' (Cavalli), 56
Egyptian Helen, The see Ägyptische Helena, Die
Elda see Loreley
Elegy for Young Lovers (Henze), 79
Elektra (R. Strauss), 11, 122, 139–140
Elisabetta, regina d'Inghilterra (Rossini), 133
Elisir d'amore, L' (Donizetti), 34, 64
Elixir of Love, The see Elisir d'amore, L'
Enfant et les sortilèges, L' (Ravel), 132
English Eccentrics (Williamson), 181
Enrico di Borgogna (Donizetti), 63
Entführung aus dem Serail, Die (Mozart), 105–106
Erismena (Cavalli), 56
Eritrea (Cavalli), 56
Ernani (Verdi), 148, 149–150
Erwartung (Schoenberg), 136
Esclarmonde (Massenet), 97
Étoile, L' (Chabrier), 56
Étoile du nord, L' (Meyerbeer), 102
Eugene Onegin (Tchaikovsky), 145–146
Euridice (Peri), 7
Euryanthe (Weber), 179
Expectation see Erwartung
Ezio (Handel), 78

Fairies, The see Feen, Die
Fair Maid of Perth, The see Jolie fille de Perth, La
Fairy Queen, The (Purcell), 131
Falce, La (Catalani), 55
False Gardener-girl, The see Finta giardiniera, La
Falstaff (Balfe), 14
Falstaff (Verdi), 42, 149, 161
Fanciulla del west, La (Puccini), 125
Faniska (Cherubini), 58
Faust (Gounod), 35, 75–76
Favola d'Orfeo, La (Monteverdi), 84, 102–103
Favorita, La (Donizetti), 67
Fedeltà premiata, La (Haydn), 78
Fedora (Giordano), 71
Feen, Die (Wagner), 161
Feigned Simpleton, The see Finta semplice, La
Feldlager in Schlesien, Ein see Étoile du nord, L'
Fennimore and Gerda (Delius), 63
Fernand Cortez (Spontini), 138
Feuersnot (R. Strauss), 138
Fidelio (Beethoven), 9, 15–18, 33
Fidelity Rewarded see Fedeltà premiata, La
Fiery Angel, The (Prokofiev), 125
Fille du régiment, La (Donizetti), 66–67
Finta giardiniera, La (Mozart), 104
Finta semplice, La (Mozart), 104
Fire Famine see Feuersnot
First the Music, then the Words see Capriccio
Fisherwomen, The see Pescatrici, Le
Fledermaus, Die (J. Strauss), 138
Fliegende Holländer, Der (Wagner), 161, 162, 167
Flying Dutchman, The see Fliegende Holländer, Der
Force of Destiny, The see Forza del destino, La
Foreign Woman, The see Straniera, La
Forza del destino, La (Verdi), 149, 157–158
Four Curmudgeons, The see Quattro rusteghi, I
Fra Diavolo (Auber), 14
Francesca da Rimini (Zandonai), 182

INDEX

Frau ohne Schatten, Die (R. Strauss), 139, 142
Freeshooter, The see Freischütz, Der
Freischütz, Der (Weber), 166, 179–180
Friedenstag (R. Strauss), 139
Friend Fritz see Amico Fritz, L'
From Day to Day see Von Heute auf Morgen
From the House of the Dead (Janáček), 88, 92

Gambler, The (Prokofiev), 125
Gazza ladra, La (Rossini), 133
Gianni Schicchi (Puccini), 125–126
Giasone (Cavalli), 56
Gioconda, La (Ponchielli), 120
Gioielli della Madonna, I (Wolf-Ferrari), 181–182
Giorno di regno, Un (Verdi), 148
Giovanna d'Arco (Verdi), 148
Giovanni Gallurese (Montemezzi), 102
Girl from Arles, The see Arlesiana, L'
Girl of the Golden West, The see Fanciulla del west, La
Giulietta e Romeo (Zandonai), 182
Giulio Cesare (Handel), 77, 78
Gloriana (Britten), 43, 51
Golden Bock, Der (Krenek), 92
Golden Cockerel, The (Rimsky-Korsakov), 132
Golden Ram, The see Goldene Bock, Der
Goldene Bock, Der (Krenek), 92
Götterdämmerung (Wagner), 162, 176–178
Greek Passion, The (Martinu), 95–96
Grande Duchesse de Gérolstein, La (Offenbach), 116
Growing Castle, The (Williamson), 181
Guillaume Tell (Rossini), 133, 135
Gunlöd (Cornelius), 61
Guntram (R. Strauss), 138
Gustave III ou Le Bal masqué (Auber), 14
Gwendoline (Chabrier), 56
Gypsy Baron, The see Zigeunerbaron, Der

Hamlet (Thomas), 147
Hänsel und Gretel (Humperdinck), 87
Hans Heiling (Marschner), 95
Happy Prince, The (Williamson), 181
Harmonie der Welt, Die (Hindemith), 82
Hélène (Saint-Saëns), 135

Hellera (Montemezzi), 102
Henry VIII (Saint-Saëns), 135
Hercules (Handel), 78
Hérodiade (Massenet), 97
Heure espagnole, L' (Ravel), 132
Hin und zurück (Hindemith), 82
Hippolyte et Aricie (Rameau), 131
Hugh the Drover (Vaughan Williams), 147
Huguenots, Les (Meyerbeer), 101–102
Human Voice, The see Voix humaine, La

Ice Break, The (Tippett), 147
Idomeneo, re di Creta (Mozart), 104–105
Impresario, The see Schauspieldirektor, Der
Incoronazione di Poppea, L' (Monteverdi), 103–104
Indes galantes, Les (Rameau), 132
Indian Queen, The (Purcell), 131
Infedeltà delusa, L' (Haydn), 78
Inquisitive Ladies, The see Donne Curiose, Le
Intermezzo (R. Strauss), 139
Intrigue and Love see Kabale und Liebe
Iphigénie en Aulide (Gluck), 73
Iphigénie en Tauride (Gluck), 73
Iris (Mascagni), 96
Isis (Lully), 95
Island God, The (Menotti), 100
Italiana in Algeri, L' (Rossini), 133
Ivanhoe see Templario, Il
Ivanhoe see Templer und die Jüdin, Der
Ivan IV (Bizet), 32
Ivan Susanin see Life for the Tsar, A

Jacobin, The (Dvořák), 68
Jean de Paris (Boieldieu), 42
Jenůfa (Janáček), 36, 88–89
Jephtha (Handel), 78
Jérusalem see Lombardi, I
Jewels of the Madonna, The see Gioielli della Madonna, I
Jewess, The see Juive, La
Jolie fille de Perth, La (Bizet), 32
Jongleur de Notre-Dame, Le (Massenet), 97
Jonny spielt auf (Krenek), 92–93
Jonny Strikes up see Jonny spielt auf
Juive, La (Halévy), 77

INDEX

Julien (Charpentier), 56
Julietta (Martinu), 95
Julius Caesar see *Giulio Cesare*
Junge Lord, Der (Henze), 80

Kabale und Liebe (Einem), 68
Karl V (Krenek), 92
Katerina Ismailova (Shostakovich), 136–137
Katya Kabanova (Janáček), 88, 89–90
Khovanshchina (Mussorgsky), 114
King Arthur (Purcell), 131
King Commanded it, The see *Roi l'a dit, Le*
King in spite of Himself, The see *Roi malgré lui, Le*
King Priam (Tippett), 124, 147
King Stag see *König Hirsch*
Kiss, The (Smetana), 137
Kluge, Die (Orff), 118
Knight of the Leopard, The (Balfe), 14
Knight of the Rose, The see *Rosenkavalier, Der*
Knot Garden, The (Tippett), 147
Koanga (Delius), 63
König Hirsch (Henze), 79
Königskinder (Humperdinck), 87

Lady Macbeth of the Mtsensk District, The see *Katerina Ismailova*
Lady of the Lake, The see *Donna del lago, La*
Lakmé (Delibes), 62–63
Last Savage, The (Menotti), 100
Leben des Orest (Krenek), 92
Legend of Orpheus, The see *Favola d'Orfeo, La*
Legend of the Invisible City of Kitezh, The (Rimsky-Korsakov), 132
Leicester, ou Le château de Kenilworth (Auber), 14
Leonore see *Fidelio*
Let's make an Opera (Britten), 43
Libertine punished, The see *Don Giovanni*
Libuše (Smetana), 137
Liebe der Danae, Die (R. Strauss), 139
Liebesverbot, Das (Wagner), 161
Life for the Tsar, A (Glinka), 72
Life of Orestes see *Leben des Orest*
Little Sweep, The see *Let's make an Opera*
Lodoiska (Cherubini), 58

Lodoletta (Mascagni), 96
Lohengrin (Wagner), 161, 165, 168–169
Lombardi alla prima crociata, I (Verdi), 148
Lombards at the First Crusade, The see *Lombardi, I*
Long Christmas Dinner, The (Hindemith), 82
Loreley (Catalani), 55
Louise (Charpentier), 34, 56–58
Love of Danae, The see *Liebe der Danae, Die*
Love of the Three Oranges, The (Prokofiev), 125
Love of Three Kings, The see *Amore dei tre re, L'*
Lowland see *Tiefland*
Lucia di Lammermoor (Donizetti), 35, 65–66
Lucio Silla (Mozart), 104
Lucrezia Borgia (Donizetti), 64–65
Luisa Miller (Verdi), 148, 150
Lulu (Berg), 23, 25–28
Lustigen Weiber von Windsor, Die (Nicolai), 116

Macbeth (Verdi), 148, 150
Madama Butterfly (Puccini), 125, 129–130
Madame Sans-gêne (Giordano), 71
Magic Flute, The see *Zauberflöte, Die*
Maid-Mistress, The see *Serva padrona, La*
Maid of Artois, The (Balfe), 14
Maid of Orleans, The (Tchaikovsky), 140
Maid of Pskov, The (Rimsky-Korsakov), 132
Makropulos Case, The (Janáček), 88, 90–92
Mala vita (Giordano), 70–71
Mamelles de Tirésias, Les (Poulenc), 117
Manon (Massenet), 97–98
Manon Lescaut (Auber), 14
Manon Lescaut (Puccini), 125
Maomotto II (Rossini), 133
Maria Golovin (Menotti), 100
Maria Stuarda (Donizetti), 65
Marriage of Figaro, The see *Nozze di Figaro, Le*
Martha (Flotow), 69–70

188

INDEX

Martyrs, Les (Donizetti), 67
Mary, Queen of Scots (Musgrave), 114
Mary Stuart see Maria Stuarda
Maschere, Le (Mascagni), 96
Masked Ball, A see Ballo in maschera, Un
Maskers, The see Maschere, Le
Masnadieri, I (Verdi), 148
Masquerade (Nielsen), 116
Master Peter's Puppet Show see Retablo de Maese Pedro, El
Mastersingers of Nuremberg, The see Meistersinger von Nürnberg, Die
Mathis der Maler (Hindemith), 82
Matrimonio segreto, Il (Cimarosa), 60
Mavra (Stravinsky), 144
May Night, A (Rimsky-Korsakov), 132
Mazeppa (Tchaikovsky), 145
Medecin malgré lui, Le (Gounod), 75
Médée (Cherubini), 58
Medici, I (Leoncavallo), 93
Medium, The (Menotti), 100
Mefistofele (Boito), 42
Meistersinger von Nürnberg, Die (Wagner), 162, 166, 171–173
Mephistopheles see Mefistofele
Merry Wives of Windsor, The see Lustigen Weiber von Windsor, Die
Midsummer Marriage, The (Tippett), 147
Midsummer Night's Dream, A (Britten), 33, 43–44
Mignon (Thomas), 147
Milton (Spontini), 138
Mireille (Gounod), 75, 76
Mr Brouček's Excursion to the Fifteenth Century (Janáček), 88
Mr Brouček's Excursion to the Moon (Janáček), 88
Mitridate, re di Ponto (Mozart), 104
Mlada (Borodin), 42–43
Mock Doctor, The see Medecin malgré lui, Le
Moïse et Pharaon see Mosè in Egitto
Mond, Der (Orff), 118
Mondo della luna, Il (Haydn), 78
Moon, The see Mond, Der
Mosè in Egitto (Rossini), 133
Moses und Aron (Schoenberg), 136
Muette de Portici, La (Auber), 14

Nabucco (Verdi), 148, 149

Nais (Rameau), 132
Navarraise, La (Massenet), 97
Nave, La (Montemezzi), 102
Nelson (Berkeley), 28
Nero (Handel), 77
Nerone (Boito), 42
Neues vom Tage (Hindemith), 82
News of the Day see Neues vom Tage
Nibelung's Ring, The see Ring des Nibelungen, Der
Night Flight see Volo di notte
Nightingale, The (Stravinsky), 144
Nonne sanglante, La (Gounod), 75
Norma (Bellini), 18, 20–22
Nose, The (Shostakovich), 136
Notte di Zoraima, La (Montemezzi), 102
Noyes Fludde (Britten), 43
Nozze di Figaro, Le (Mozart), 84, 106–108

Oberon (Weber), 180
Oberto (Verdi), 148
Oca del Cairo, L' (Mozart), 104
Oedipus Rex (Stravinsky), 144
Olympians, The (Bliss), 28
Olympie (Spontini), 138
Oprichnik, The (Tchaikovsky), 145
Orfeo ed Euridice (Gluck), 73–74
Orlando (Handel), 78
Ormindo, L' (Cavalli), 56
Orphée aux enfers (Offenbach), 116
Orpheus and Eurydice see Orfeo ed Euridice
Orpheus in the Underworld see Orphée aux enfers
Otello (Rossini), 133
Otello (Verdi), 42, 149, 160–161, 164
Our Lady's Juggler see Jongleur de Notre-Dame, Le
Our Man in Havana (Williamson), 181
Owen Wingrave (Britten), 44

Pagliacci (Leoncavallo), 93, 94
Palestrina (Pfitzner), 119
Pallas Athene weint (Krenek), 92
Pallas Athene wept see Pallas Athene weint
Pardon de Ploërmel, Le (Meyerbeer), 102
Paride e Elena (Gluck), 73
Paris and Helen see Paride e Elena
Parsifal (Wagner), 162, 178–179

INDEX

Paul Bunyan (Britten), 43
Pearl Fishers, The see Pêcheurs de perles, Les
Peasant and the Rogue, The (Dvořák), 68
Pêcheurs de perles, Les (Bizet), 32, 37–38
Pelléas et Mélisande (Debussy), 62
Pénélope (Fauré), 69
Périchole, La (Offenbach), 116
Perfect Fool, The (Holst), 87
Pescatrici, Le (Haydn), 78
Phryné (Saint-Saëns), 135
Piccolo Marat, Il (Mascagni), 96
Pierre et Catherine (Adam), 13
Pietra del paragone, La (Rossini), 133
Pilgrim's Progress, The (Vaughan Williams), 148
Pirata, Il (Bellini), 18
Poacher, The see Wildschütz, Der
Poisoned Kiss, The (Vaughan Williams), 148
Poliuto (Donizetti), 67
Porgy and Bess (Gershwin), 70
Postillon de Longjumeau, Le (Adam), 13
Pré aux clercs, Le (Hérold), 81
Prigioniero, Il (Dallapiccola), 61–62
Prigioner superbo, Il (Pergolesi), 119
Prima la musica, e poi le parole (Salieri), 143
Prince Igor (Borodin), 43
Princesse jaune, La (Saint-Saëns), 135
Prinz von Homburg, Der (Henze), 79
Prise de Troie, La (Berlioz), 30–31
Prisoner, The see Prigioniero, Il
Prodigal Son, The (Britten), 44
Promessi sposi, I (Ponchielli), 120
Prométhée (Fauré), 69
Prophète, Le (Meyerbeer), 102
Proserpine (Lully), 95
Prozess, Der (Einem), 68
Puritani, I (Bellini), 18, 22
Puritans, The see Puritani, I

Quattro rusteghi, I (Wolf-Ferrari), 181
Queen of Spades, The (Tchaikovsky), 145, 146–147

Radamisto (Handel), 77
Rake's Progress, The (Stravinsky), 144–145

Rape of Lucretia, The (Britten), 43, 46–47
Rare Thing, A see Cosa rara, Una
Re, Il (Giordano), 71
Renard (Stravinsky), 144
Re pastore, Il (Mozart), 104
Resurrection see Risurrezione
Retablo de Maese Pedro, El (Falla), 69
Return Home of Ulysses, The see Ritorno d'Ulisse in patria, Il
Rheingold (Wagner), 162, 173
Richard Coeur-de-lion (Grétry), 77
Riders to the Sea (Vaughan Williams), 148
Rienzi (Wagner), 161
Rigoletto (Verdi), 148, 150–151
Rinaldo (Handel), 77
Ring des Nibelungen, Der (Wagner), 162, 173–178
Ring des Polykrates, Der (Korngold), 92
Rise and Fall of the City of Mahagonny see Aufstieg und Fall der Stadt Mahagonny
Risurrezione (Alfano), 13
Ritorno d'Ulisse in patria, Il (Monteverdi), 103
Ritter Pasman (J. Strauss), 138
Robert le diable (Meyerbeer), 101
Robert the Devil see Robert le diable
Roberto Devereux (Donizetti), 65
Rodelinda (Handel), 77
Rodrigo (Handel), 77
Roi de Lahore, Le (Massenet), 97
Roi d'Ys, Le (Lalo), 93
Roi l'a dit, Le (Delibes), 62
Roi malgré lui, Le (Chabrier), 56
Roland von Berlin, Der (Leoncavallo), 93, 94
Roméo et Juliette (Gounod), 75, 76
Rondine, La (Puccini), 125
Rosenkavalier, Der (R. Strauss), 139, 140–141
Royal Children, The see Königskinder
Rustic Chivalry see Cavalleria rusticana
Ruth (Berkeley), 28
Rusalka (Dvořák), 68
Russlan and Ludmila (Glinka), 72–73

Sadko (Rimsky-Korsakov), 132
Saint of Bleecker Street, The (Menotti), 100

INDEX

Salome (R. Strauss), 138, 139
Samson (Handel), 78
Samson et Dalila (Saint-Saëns), 135–136
Sapho (Gounod), 75
Sapho (Massenet), 97
Saul (Handel), 78
Saul and David (Nielsen), 116
Savitri (Holst), 87
Schauspieldirektor, Der (Mozart), 104
Schweigsame Frau, Die (R. Strauss), 123, 139
Scipione Affricano (Cavalli), 56
Secret, The (Smetana), 137
Secret Marriage, The see *Matrimonio segreto, Il*
Segreto di Susanna, Il (Wolf-Ferrari), 181
Semele (Handel), 78
Semiramide (Rossini), 133
Serse (Handel), 78
Serva padrona, La (Pergolesi), 8, 119
Shepherd King, The see *Re pastore, Il*
Shvanda the Bagpiper (Weinberger), 181
Siberia (Giordano), 71
Sicilian Vespers, The see *Vêpres siciliennes, Les*
Siège de Corinthe, Le (Rossini), 133
Siege of Rochelle, The (Balfe), 14
Siegfried (Wagner), 162, 175–176
Silent Woman, The see *Schweigsame Frau, Die*
Simon Boccanegra (Verdi), 148, 154–155, 164
Sir John in Love (Vaughan Williams), 148
Sleepwalker, The see *Sonnambula, La*
Sly (Wolf-Ferrari), 182
Snow Maiden, The (Rimsky-Korsakov), 132
Sogno di Scipione, Il (Mozart), 104
Soldaten, Die (Zimmermann), 182
Soldiers, The see *Soldaten, Die*
Sonnambula, La (Bellini), 18–20
Sorceress, The (Tchaikovsky), 145
Sorochintsy Fair (Mussorgsky), 114
Spanish Hour, The see *Heure espagnole, L'*
Speziale, Lo (Haydn), 78
Sposo deluso, Lo (Mozart), 104
Star of the North, The see *Étoile du nord, L'*
Stiffelio (Verdi), 148

Story of Gösta Berling, The see *Cavalieri di Ekebù, I*
Story of Tsar Saltan (Rimsky-Korsakov), 132
Straniera, La (Bellini), 18
Suor Angelica (Puccini), 125–126
Susanna's Secret see *Segreto di Susanna, Il*
Swallow, The see *Rondine, La*

Tabarro, Il (Puccini), 125–126
Tales of Hoffmann, The see *Contes d'Hoffmann, Les*
Talismano, Il see *Knight of the Leopard, The*
Tancredi (Rossini), 133
Tannhäuser (Wagner), 161, 167–168
Tante Aurore (Boieldieu), 42
Telephone, The (Menotti), 100
Tempest, The (Purcell), 131
Templario, Il (Nicolai), 116
Templer und die Jüdin, Der (Marschner), 95
Thaïs (Massenet), 97, 99
There and Back see *Hin und zurück*
Thérèse (Massenet), 97
Thésée (Lully), 95
Thieving Magpie, The see *Gazza ladra, La*
Thomas and Sally (Arne), 13
Threepenny Opera, The see *Dreigroschenoper, Die*
Three Pintos, The see *Drei Pintos, Die*
Tiefland (D'Albert), 61
Tobias and the Angel (Bliss), 41
Tosca (Puccini), 125, 127–129
Tote Stadt, Die (Korngold), 92
Touchstone, The see *Pietra del paragone, La*
Traviata, La (Verdi), 148, 153–154, 163
Trial, The see *Prozess, Der*
Trionfi dell'Afrodite (Orff), 118
Tristan und Isolde (Wagner), 161–162, 169–171
Trittico, Il (Puccini), 125–126
Troilus and Cressida (Walton), 179
Trojans, The see *Troyens, Les*
Troubadour, The see *Trovatore, Il*
Trovatore, Il (Verdi), 148, 151–153
Troyens, Les (Berlioz), 29, 30–32
Tsar and Carpenter see *Zar und Zimmermann*

191

INDEX

Tsar's Bride, The (Rimsky-Korsakov), 132
Tsar's Bride, The (Borodin), 42
Turandot (Busoni), 55
Turandot (Puccini), 13, 126, 130–131
Turco in Italia, Il (Rossini), 133
Turn of the Screw, The (Britten), 43, 51–53
Twilight of the Gods, The see *Götterdämmerung*
Two Widows, The (Smetana), 137

Ulisse (Dallapiccola), 62
Undine (Lortzing), 95

Vakula the Smith (Tchaikovsky), 145
Valkyrie, The see *Walküre, Die*
Vampyr, Der (Marschner), 95
Vanessa (Barber), 14
Venus and Adonis (Blow), 41–42
Vêpres siciliennes, Les (Verdi), 148
Vestale, La (Spontini), 138
Vida breve, La (Falla), 69
Vie parisienne, La (Offenbach), 116
Village Romeo and Juliet, A (Delius), 63
Violanta (Korngold), 92
Visit of the Old Lady, The see *Besuch der alten Dame, Der*
Vixen Sharpears see *Cunning Little Vixen, The*
Voice of Ariadne, The (Musgrave), 114
Voix humaine, La (Poulenc), 120
Volo di notte (Dallapiccola), 61
Von Heute auf Morgen (Schoenberg), 136

Voyevoda, The (Tchaikovsky), 145

Wally, La (Catalani), 56
Walküre, Die (Wagner), 162, 173–175
Wandering Scholar, The (Holst), 87
War and Peace (Prokofiev), 125
Water Carrier, The see *Deux journées, Les*
We Come to the River (Henze), 36, 80–81
Werther (Massenet), 97, 98–99
White Lady, The see *Dame blanche, La*
Wildschütz, Der (Lortzing), 94–95
William Tell see *Guillaume Tell*
Woman without a Shadow, The see *Frau ohne Schatten, Die*
World of the Moon, The see *Mondo della luna, Il*
Wozzeck (Berg), 23–25

Xerse (Cavalli), 56
Xerxes see *Serse*

Yolanta (Tchaikovsky), 145
Young Lord, The see *Junge Lord, Der*

Zaïde (Mozart), 104
Zaira (Bellini), 18
Zampa (Hérold), 81
Zar und Zimmermann (Lortzing), 94
Zauberflöte, Die (Mozart), 111–113
Zazà (Leoncavallo), 93
Zémire et Azor (Grétry), 77
Zigeunerbaron, Der (J. Strauss), 138
Zoroastre (Rameau), 132
Zwingburg (Krenek), 92